THE
EVIL MADNESS OF
HITLER

THE
EVIL MADNESS OF
HITLER

THE DAMNING PSYCHIATRIC PROFILE

NIGEL CAWTHORNE

This edition published in 2022 by Arcturus Publishing Limited
26/27 Bickels Yard, 151–153 Bermondsey Street,
London SE1 3HA

AD010604UK

Printed in the UK

CONTENTS

Introduction

Adolf Hitler has been dead for more than seventy-five years. He committed some of the most appalling crimes ever wreaked on humanity and dragged the world into the most destructive war in history. He even destroyed Germany, the country he purported to love. As the Allies invaded the Reich he once said would last for a thousand years, he ordered the destruction of the remaining infrastructure, because he believed that the German people were not worthy of him.

Appearing much older than his fifty-six years, he died an ignominious death, killing himself with a pistol while Eva Braun, his wife of one day, took cyanide. Many thought him a madman, though chillingly he was fully aware of his unique ruthlessness and brutality – making his behaviour even more inexcusable and repellent. Yet, decades after his death, there are still people – not just in Germany, but also in the United States and Russia, a country that lost so many to defeat him – who idolize him.

Even those who despise Hitler and his philosophy are fascinated. The publishing industry continues to turn out more books about him than almost any other figure in history. Films and TV documentaries are constantly being made about him. We still try to understand how a man who had been barely more than a derelict, living in hostels for the homeless before becoming a soldier of little distinction, could rise to unprecedented power in one of the most civilized countries in the world and persuade its people to march into the abyss with him.

World War II did not come about by accident. A number of the defendants at the Nuremberg Trials of war criminals in 1945–46 were convicted of beginning a war of aggression – they had been at meetings where Hitler had made it perfectly clear that he intended to go to war.

It was already plain that the man was unhinged. The world had seen his ranting speeches in the newsreels and heard them on the radio. They made no sense other than to those caught up in his fervour. To the outside observer it was clear that, more than any other figure in modern times, Hitler was living out his own pathological psychodrama on the world stage. Hundreds of millions would be caught up in it; many millions died.

Even while the war was in progress, attempts were made to ascertain what was going on in his mind. Curiously, he had spent his early years as a down and out in Vienna, a city that was also home to Sigmund Freud, who in the early years of the twentieth century was advancing the discipline of psychoanalysis, which sought to unlock the understanding of the unconscious mind. This quickly became a dominant force in psychology and psychiatry.

When Hitler and the Nazis took over Austria in the *Anschluss* of 1938, Freud, a Jew, was forced to flee to England where he died the following year, just three weeks after the outbreak of war. However, his understanding of the human psyche had not died with him. Across the Atlantic, academics at Harvard used his techniques in an attempt to fathom Hitler's pathology. These are Hitler's psychiatric files.

Nigel Cawthorne
Bloomsbury

PSYCHOBIOGRAPHY OF ADOLF HITLER

Presenting symptoms	Deep-seated unconscious obsession with imposing system of order as means of achieving absolute power
Reasons behind obsessive compulsive elements	Individual whose power-seeking behaviour is compensation for inner doubts and low self-esteem
Relationship with mother/father	Indulgent mother/harsh authoritarian father
Empathy with the nation of Germany	Visionary goals, articulated in language of moralistic oratory, chime with the national mood in Germany, demanding restoration of order and national unity
Unusual/abnormal/ pathological personality traits	Paranoia, megalomania, isolation, ill health, social isolation, vegetarian!!

Rudolf Hess stands next to SA commander Viktor Lutze as Hitler takes the salute during the 1938 Party Conference.

CHAPTER 1

Hitler: Man and Monster

The twentieth century had more than its fair share of monstrous tyrants. There were plenty of petty despots too, including Francisco Franco in Spain, Benito Mussolini in Italy, 'Papa Doc' Duvalier in Haiti, Idi Amin in Uganda, Augusto Pinochet in Chile, Pol Pot in Cambodia and Colonel Mengistu Haile Mariam in Ethiopia. But however numerous their crimes, they hardly made it into the major league as challengers to Hitler.

When it comes to killing, the worst offender, without a doubt, was China's Mao Zedong. After coming to power in China in 1949, he systematically executed those he considered 'class enemies' and throughout his long tenure of power he ruthlessly eliminated his political rivals. Millions were sent to labour camps where they were worked to death.

In his Great Leap Forward, which ran from 1958 to 1961, he forcibly collectivized agriculture and decided that to become an economic power China must make steel. Everyone must contribute by building smelting shops in their own backyards. Short of raw materials, people had to render pots and agricultural tools to meet quotas. As a result at least eighteen million people starved to death.

This was followed by the Cultural Revolution of 1966–76. The Revolution unleashed the Red Guards, militant university and high-school students who sought to root out counter-revolutionaries – which turned out to be anyone they disagreed with. Then, in the Down to the Countryside Movement, privileged young city dwellers were forced out into the fields to become farmers. Again untold millions died. It is estimated that Mao was responsible for the deaths of some sixty million people.

Joseph Stalin probably killed around forty million human beings. He deliberately created a famine in Ukraine by confiscating food stocks, killed the wealthier peasants, known as kulaks, purged his own party by having thousands shot, moved whole populations he considered disloyal to remote regions, where they starved, and consigned millions to the Gulags, a chain of labour camps in the Arctic regions. Few returned.

Adolf Hitler is thought to come third in the league of mass murderers. But there was something peculiarly appalling about his most notorious crime, the Holocaust. Although there exists no single document, signed by Hitler, ordering the extermination of the Jews, it is clear from his speeches and writings, and the testimony of those who went on to carry out the policy, that his wishes were being followed. It is still hard to comprehend to this day. He also unleashed a war that consumed Europe and, ultimately, the whole world.

PATH TO POWER

Of these three tyrants, it is Hitler that continues to fascinate. He is uniquely difficult to understand. Mao and Stalin can be dismissed as falling into the mould of Chinese or Russian despots, ruling relatively backward countries with a rod of iron, and that was how they saw themselves. But Hitler was different. He saw himself as the saviour of the German nation, though he was not himself German. Born in Austria in 1889, he only became a German citizen in 1932 while running in the presidential election. The following year he became chancellor.

True, Stalin was a Georgian, not a Russian, but Georgia had been part of the Russian Empire since 1801. It was briefly independent under British protection from 1918 to 1920, but by that time Stalin was already a member of the Central Committee in Petrograd, now St Petersburg.

Mao and Stalin were almost Marxists – of sorts. No matter how brutal their methods, they ostensibly sought to introduce the communist philosophy of the nineteenth-century revolutionary and economist Karl Marx, who also attracted peaceful adherents. Hitler's philosophy was entirely his own. It was spelt out in the book *Mein Kampf* – 'My Struggle'.

Joseph Stalin at Yalta in 1945: Stalin was a typical Russian despot, ruling a backward country with a rod of iron.

This was published in two volumes in 1925 and 1927 and made him a rich man. The first volume was called *Eine Abrechnung*, which has been translated variously as 'The Reckoning' or 'Revenge'.

It must be remembered that unlike Mao Zedong and Stalin, Hitler was elected to office. He first tried to seize power through the Munich Beer Hall Putsch in 1923. This failed and earned him nine months in jail. After that he resolved to take power by legal means. In the 1930 election to the German parliament, the Reichstag, the Nazi Party took 107 seats, making it the second-largest party in the assembly. In the elections in July 1932, the Nazis took 230 seats. And in the presidential election that September, running against Field Marshal Paul von Hindenburg, Hitler took 36.8 per cent of the vote on the second ballot. Two months later, on 30 January 1933, Hindenburg made him chancellor of a short-lived coalition.

Hitler quickly set about establishing an absolute dictatorship. Within a month, on 27 February, there was a fire at the Reichstag which was blamed on Dutch communist Marinus van der Lubbe. He was quickly tried and executed, while all personal rights and freedoms were suspended, detention without trial was permitted and four thousand members of the Communist Party were arrested.

On 5 March there were fresh elections, where the Nazis took 43.9 per cent of the vote and 288 seats in the Reichstag, with their Nationalist partners taking another 8 per cent and 52 seats, giving the coalition a majority. At a meeting in the Kroll Opera House, the German parliament passed the Enabling Act, giving Hitler full powers to enact laws without the consent of the Reichstag. Less than three months later, all non-Nazi parties, organizations and trade unions were banned. In the elections that November, the Nazis took 92 per cent of the vote and all 661 seats in the Reichstag. After that, the parliament met only to ratify Hitler's decisions by a unanimous vote and to listen to his speeches.

The following July, in the Night of the Long Knives, Hitler ordered that members of rival factions in the Nazi Party be rounded up and shot. On 2 August, the day of Hindenburg's death, Hitler combined the offices of chancellor and president, although this was forbidden by Article 2 of the Enabling Act. No one objected. A plebiscite was called on the same day, in order to gain public approval. When the German people went to

Hitler bows to Hindenburg in Berlin, 1934. The pose was designed to give the impression he was no threat to the established order.

the polls on the 19th, a vote of 90 per cent was recorded, approving the combination of the two offices.

As head of state, Hitler became supreme commander of the armed forces. Each member of the military had to swear a personal oath of loyalty to Hitler himself, by name, not just to the state. He then took one of the most civilized nations in the world and plunged it into a barbarism not seen since the Dark Ages.

UNLIKELY CANDIDATE

History tells us how he managed to do this politically, but it does not explain the forces that drove him to do it. On the face of it, he seemed such an unlikely candidate to become one of the great monsters of modern times. In early life, he was ordinary and unprepossessing to an extraordinary degree. Born to a working-class family in a provincial town, he was an insipid child and did poorly at school. He fancied himself an artist, but showed little talent.

Unwilling to work, he became a down and out. Below average height, his hips were wide and his shoulders narrow. His legs were short and spindly, his muscles flabby and he had a hollow chest. In later life, he had the tunic of his uniform padded. He certainly would not have reached the physical standards required to join his own elite bodyguard.

He was too weak to be employed on construction work and was rejected as unfit by the Austrian army at the outbreak of World War I. In Munich, he joined the 16th Bavarian Reserve Infantry Regiment. Like millions of others, he did his duty during the war, though he never rose in rank beyond corporal.

Those who knew him after the war commented on his poor state of personal hygiene. His teeth were rotten and he had long, dirty fingernails. The clothes he wore – whether an anonymous blue suit or the Bavarian costume of a white shirt, leather shorts and braces – were none too clean and his hair, then dark brown and parted in the middle, was plastered down against his scalp with oil. His voice often broke into a shrill falsetto and his physical movements were described as 'womanish'.

According to Harvard psychologist Henry A. Murray, in a report to the Office of Strategic Services (OSS) in October 1943, Hitler had 'a dainty, ladylike way of walking (when not assuming a military carriage in public), effeminate gestures of the arms – a peculiar graceless ineptitude reminiscent of a girl throwing a baseball'.

'Every few steps he cocked his right shoulder nervously, his left leg snapping up as he did so,' said Dr Walter Langer in another OSS report. 'He also had a tic in his face which caused the corner of his lips to curl upwards.'

American journalist Edgar Mowrer, seeing Hitler for the first time at the trial following the unsuccessful Beer Hall Putsch in Munich in 1923, said: 'Was this provincial dandy, with his slick dark hair, his cutaway coat, his awkward gestures and glib tongue, the terrible rebel? He seemed for all the world like a travelling salesman for a clothing firm.'

Meeting Hitler for the first time in 1931, Dorothy Thompson wrote in *Harper's Magazine*:

'He is formless, almost faceless, a man whose countenance is a caricature, a man whose framework seems cartilaginous, without bones. He is inconsequent and voluble, ill poised and insecure. He is the very prototype of the little man.'

And it was not just Americans looking down on Hitler because he did not match up to the New World's muscular ideal of masculine beauty. Professor Max von Gruber, a leading proponent of 'racial hygiene', testifying in 1923, said:

'It was the first time I had seen Hitler close at hand. Face and head of inferior type, cross-breed; low receding forehead, ugly nose, broad cheekbones, little eyes, dark hair. Expression not of a man exercising authority in perfect self-command, but of raving excitement. At the end an expression of satisfied egotism.'

HYPNOTIC EYES

However, many people commented on his eyes. They were a bright blue, bordering on violet – though people who met him described them as almost every colour of the rainbow. But it was not their colour that was important, but rather their depth and glint which gave them a hypnotic quality. A typical story was related by a policeman who had no Nazi sympathies, but had been stationed at the entrance to the Berlin Sportpalast where a rally was being held. When Hitler arrived, he took the policeman to be a bodyguard assigned for his personal protection. He strutted up to him and grabbed his hand. While holding it in what was said to be 'his famous, straight-forward, he-man grip', he gazed into the police officer's eyes with that fatal hypnotizing and irresistible glare, which swept the poor officer right off his feet.

Clicking to attention, he told his police chief the following morning: 'Since last night I am a National Socialist. Heil Hitler!'

What picked Hitler out was that he was a charismatic speaker. He spoke in a strange mixture of High German and Austrian dialect. By any normal standard, his speeches were agonizingly long, badly structured and excruciatingly repetitious. They make painful reading. But it was his delivery that captivated his audiences.

He was never the first to speak, always having someone to warm up the audience for him. As he came to power, he became the showman. He scheduled his speeches for late in the evening when the audience would be tired and their resistance low. At the critical moment, Hitler would emerge through a door at the back of the hall. With a small group of henchmen behind him, he would march between two columns of uniformed storm troopers, looking neither left nor right, while a military band would play. No one would be allowed to accost him or speak to him.

Then he began, haltingly at first. He seemed nervous and unable to think of anything to say. But then, as he got a feel for his audience, he took off. In that transformation from ordinary little man to soaring orator, he took his audience with him.

The German people had never seen anything like it. A German journalist said: 'He was a man transformed and possessed. We were in the presence of a miracle.'

The themes were always the same – the 'November criminals' who had signed the Armistice in 1918, the Marxist enemy and the world domination of the Jews. His rant became practically hysterical. As in a Wagnerian aria it was almost as if he was surging towards a sexual climax and would only stop when he was completely exhausted and drenched with sweat.

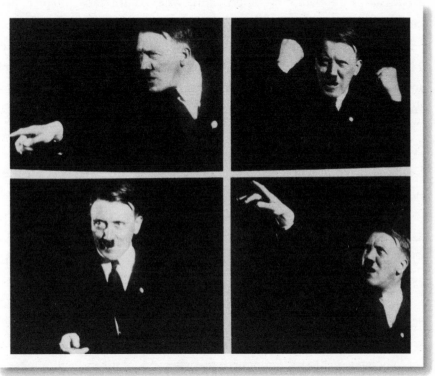

Nazi photographer Heinrich Hoffmann took thousands of photos of Hitler, including these ones of him rehearsing his speeches.

In his autobiographical treatise *Mein Kampf*, Hitler explained the rationale that lay behind his speeches:

'The psyche of the broad masses does not respond to anything weak or halfway. Like a woman, whose spiritual sensitivity is determined less by abstract reason than by an indefinable emotional longing for fulfilling power and who, for that reason, prefers to submit to the strong rather than the weakling – the mass, too, prefers the ruler to the pleader.'

Newsweek reported: 'Women faint, when, with face purpled and contorted with effort, he blows forth his magic oratory.'

It certainly had that effect on one woman, American writer Janet Flanner, who said: 'His oratory used to wilt his collar, unglue his forelock, glaze his eyes; he was like a man hypnotized, repeating himself into a frenzy.'

'When, at the climax, he sways from one side to the other, his listeners sway with him,' wrote another observer, 'when he leans forward they also lean forward and when he concludes they either are awed and silent or on their feet in a frenzy.'

UNCANNY INTUITION

Otto Strasser, an early follower of Hitler, explained his extraordinary power as a speaker.

'I can only attribute it to his uncanny intuition, which infallibly diagnoses the ills from which his audience are suffering. If he tries to bolster up his argument with theories or quotations from books he has only imperfectly understood, he scarcely rises above a very poor mediocrity. But let him throw away the crutches and step out boldly, speaking as the spirit moves him, and he is promptly transformed into one of the greatest speakers of the century.'

Strasser noted that Hitler made no attempt to prove his assertions and was strongest when he spoke of abstractions such as honour, country, nation, family, and loyalty.

Hitler nurtured his personal image with great care to ensure that his adoring public perceived him to be the father figure of the nation.

Hitler also used phrases that would make an educated person blush with their triteness:

> 'but spoken by Hitler, they inflame the audience, they go straight to every heart ... His words go like an arrow to their target, he touches each private wound on the raw, liberating the mass unconscious, expressing its innermost aspirations, telling it what it wants to hear.'

The effect was most marked with women. At the Nuremberg Congress of 1936, he addressed an audience of twenty thousand women. According to Strasser:

> 'They were old and young, ugly and beautiful, married, spinsters and widows, embittered and hopeful, worried and lonely, of respectable morals or otherwise. Hitler knows nothing of woman or of women; yet to his lips there sprang a phrase that provoked delirious enthusiasm: "What have I given you? What has National-Socialism given you? We have given you Man!" The response of the audience can only be described as orgiastic.'

He also said that it would be wrong to think that Hitler had always been an unscrupulous demagogue.

'He was at one time genuinely convinced of the rightness of his cause,' said Strasser. 'He believes what he says; carried away by a mystical force, he cannot doubt the genuineness of his mission.'

Strasser, who joined the Nazi Party in 1925, watched Hitler's transformation into the all-powerful Führer:

> 'He began by being the Unknown Soldier who had survived the war. A moving and obscure hero, he shed real tears for his country's misfortunes. Soon he discovered that his lachrymatory glands were obliging and could be turned on at will. After that he wept to the point of excess. Next he was St John the Baptist, preparing himself for the coming of the Messiah; then the Messiah

Hitler meeting some enthusiastic young female supporters. The Hitler Myth created by Goebbels was so successful that many Germans who encountered the Führer immediately began to swoon.

himself, pending his appearance in the role of Caesar. One day he realized the shattering effect of his rages; henceforth rage and abuse were the favourite weapons in his armoury.'

Next came Hitler's unshakeable belief in himself. As editor of the newspaper *Der Nationalsozialist* in Berlin, Strasser found himself in dispute with Hitler. According to Strasser, Hitler had been advancing an untenable argument for half an hour, when Strasser said to him: 'But you are mistaken, Herr Hitler.'

'He fixed me with a stare and exclaimed in a fury: "I cannot be mistaken. What I do and say is historical,"' Strasser recalled.

Then Hitler fell silent and left without another word. Strasser turned to his brother and said: 'Gregor, the man's a megalomaniac.'

For Otto Strasser this was a key event.

'That day the dogma of Hitler's infallibility was born,' he said.

Writer and politician Otto Strasser was one of the people who understood Hitler's deep joylessness and lack of humour.

POWER FOR ITS OWN SAKE

Then there was Hitler's belief in power for its own sake. Otto and Gregor Strasser were on the left wing of the Nazi Party, before Hitler moved it to the right at the behest of industrialists. They believed in the nationalization of the banks and industry, social reform and closer ties with the Soviet Union. At that time, Hitler had no constructive agenda and Strasser recalled their first quarrel.

> "'Power!' screamed Hitler. "We must have power!" "Before we gain it," I replied firmly, "let us decide what we propose to do with it. Our programme is too vague; we must construct something solid and enduring." Hitler, who even then could hardly bear contradiction, thumped the table and barked: "Power first! Afterwards we can act as circumstances dictate."

While Hitler claimed to be decisive, he hesitated over minor decisions, claiming pressure of work. Otto Strasser recalled an occasion where, after endless procrastination, Hitler met his brother in a restaurant. When Gregor then raised the issue, Hitler slipped out of a side door, sending his chauffeur back later to get his hat and coat.

Hitler did not surround himself with friends but with accomplices – pimps, crooks and killers, who called him 'Adi', slapped him on the back and even dared to tell smutty stories in front of him.

'Hitler enjoys their company, for they confirm his profound conviction that man is essentially vile,' said Strasser.

Discussing Machiavelli with him, Hitler said: 'Man is congenitally evil. He can only be controlled by force. To govern him everything is permissible. You must lie, betray, even kill when policy demands it. ... That morality is only valid for men born to command. It gives them the right to act as masters.'

'What joy can a man like Hitler find in life?' asked Strasser. 'He loves no one. He does not even enjoy nature, and his eyes see nothing of its beauty. He rarely smiles, and is denied the gift of humour, that divine gift that enables men to laugh even at themselves.'

Hitler himself said: 'I follow my course with the precision and security of a sleepwalker.'

Strasser commented:

'Yes, but the sleepwalker has no desire to see clearly. Systematic thinking, and above all criticism, are hateful to him. He has no ideas, and no true ideals. He advances blindly, guided by that extraordinary flair which has made him what he is. He hates intelligence, and he is tormented by the sense of his own inferiority. ...

'In his speeches words such as hate, destruction, fanaticism constantly recur; but one searches vainly for words such as love, cultivate, sprout, bud, grow. He is a slave of technique and seems to have no conception of organic evolution. The miracle of creation, the mystery of birth are unknown to him. He has never had children, nor the hope of them. The privilege of creating the simplest and most beautiful thing in the world was denied him. What does he know of life?'

Even Hitler's famed asceticism was purely materialistic.

'He believes that meat is unhealthy, that smoking is poisonous, and that drink lulls one's vigilance,' said Strasser. 'He would consider it a supreme disgrace to drop his guard.'

One day Strasser suggested to him that 'a good German dictator should teach the German people to appreciate subtlety in cooking and in love'.

Hitler hissed through clenched teeth in contempt: 'You cynic! You sybarite.'

'It was useless to explain to him that the gods of antiquity loved women and wine none the less for being heroes,' said Strasser. 'This kind of reflection appalled Hitler, who always fought shy of the slightest allusion to or hint of suggestiveness.'

Otto Strasser eventually concluded that Hitler was a monster. He was expelled from the Nazi Party and set up his own party, called the Black Front. Gregor Strasser was killed during the Night of the Long Knives in 1934. Otto escaped, eventually settling in Canada. Throughout the war, he wrote articles about the Nazi leadership. Propaganda Minister Joseph Goebbels dubbed him 'Public Enemy Number One' and there was a price of $500,000 on his head.

As an unreformed National Socialist, Strasser was not allowed to return to Germany until 1955. He died there in 1974.

CHAPTER 2
Attempts at Understanding

At first Hitler was not taken very seriously outside
Germany. Short in stature with a toothbrush moustache,
he resembled 'the Tramp', the comic figure Charlie
Chaplin had been playing in films since 1914, taking
him to worldwide fame. There were other similarities
between Chaplin and Hitler. They had been born just
four days apart and both had risen from poverty to world
prominence. Chaplin was also interested in politics,
but was of a distinctly left-wing persuasion. Later he
was suspected of being a communist and was denied
a permit to re-enter the United States in 1952.

Chaplin had seen Leni Riefenstahl's 1935 Nazi propaganda film *Triumph
of the Will*, chronicling the 1934 Nazi Party Congress in Nuremberg. Its
ranks of storm troopers filled many who saw it with fear, but Chaplin
laughed and set to work on his film *The Great Dictator*, satirizing
Hitler and Italian Fascist leader Benito Mussolini. The film went into
production in Los Angeles in September 1939, six days after World War
II broke out. This was a bold move and the United States was at that
time neutral. In the film, Chaplin's Little Tramp became a persecuted
Jewish barber; Chaplin also played the dictator Adenoid Hynkel, using
mannerisms and gestures he had picked up from studying newsreels.
The intention was clear. The *Chicago Sun-Times* said that Chaplin 'put
the Little Tramp and $1.5 million of his own money on the line to
ridicule Hitler'.

The Great Dictator: Chaplin said he would not have made this film if he had understood the full extent of Hitler's monstrousness.

Released in October 1940, *The New York Times* called *The Great Dictator* 'the most eagerly awaited picture of the year'. It received five Academy Award nominations, including Best Picture, Best Original Screenplay and Best Actor. Chaplin was afraid that wartime audiences might not welcome a comedy about a dictator they had every reason to fear and hate, but it made $11 million worldwide, becoming Chaplin's highest grossing film.

Serious attempts to understand Hitler were also being made. One came from former Nazi Party member Dr Hermann Rauschning, who became president of the senate in Danzig, now Gdańsk, in 1933 and resigned from the senate and the Nazi Party in 1934. Opposing the Nazis at the next election, he found himself in danger and fled. In Britain in 1939, he published *Hitler Speaks: A Series of Political Conversations with Adolf Hitler on his Real Aims*; *Germany's Revolution of Destruction*; and *The Beast from the Abyss*. The *Daily Express* billed him as 'The Man Who Knows Hitler's Mind' and published a series of articles by him. However, Rauschning was a politician and a historian and gave no real insight into Hitler's psychological condition.

In London in 1940, P. Callon Humphreys published *Mind of a Tyrant: A Psychological Study of the Character of Hitler*. This employed the language of psychoanalysis to examine Hitler and compared him repeatedly to a homicidal psychopath in Düsseldorf who strangled his victims during the sexual act. At just thirty-one pages, it was neither very thorough nor particularly enlightening.

CASE NOTES

However, in the autumn of 1941, before America had even entered the war, Harvard psychology student W.H.D. Vernon began writing 'Hitler the Man – Notes for a Case History' under the supervision of Professor Henry A. Murray and Professor Gordon W. Allport. (Professor Murray would submit his own report to the OSS in October 1943.) It was published in the *Journal of Abnormal and Social Psychology* in July 1942 and begins:

'The purpose of this paper is to bring together in brief form what is known about Adolf Hitler as a man. For if the strategists could peer "inside Hitler" and adapt their strategy to what they find there, it is likely that the winning of the war would be speeded.'

However, Vernon admitted that 'the intricacies of so complex a personality would be difficult enough to unravel were the subject present and co-operating in the task'.

Much of the reporting on Hitler was far from objective and presented 'very inadequate psychological data', which made the task even more difficult. Nevertheless, 'as primary source material, Hitler's own writings and speeches … tell us a good deal', Vernon wrote, though any evaluation could only be tentative.

'In any case study, one must begin by asking who the subject is, whence he came, who were his forebears,' said Vernon. He decided that *Hitler: A Biography* by Konrad Heiden, an influential Jewish journalist from Munich, provided the most reliable genealogy available. Heiden's biography was published in two volumes in Zürich in 1936 and 1937. He escaped to the United States in 1940.

However, Heiden himself pointed out that he was uncertain about the details of Hitler's family as they were collected from stray publications and that Hitler was reticent about his background to the point of arousing suspicion that he had something to hide. Nevertheless, Vernon went on to give a whistle-stop account of what was then known of Hitler's ancestry and early life.

ANCESTRY

Hitler's father, Alois, was born the illegitimate son of Maria Anna Schicklgruber in 1837 in the village of Strones in Lower Austria. He was thought to be the son of Johann Georg Hiedler. Until his fortieth year, Alois bore the name Schicklgruber. It was not until thirty-five years after the death of his mother and nineteen years after the death of Johann Georg Hiedler that Alois took his name, using the alternative spelling, 'Hitler'.

Heiden said:

'In the life history of Adolf Hitler no mention is ever made of the grandparents on his father's side; the details invariably refer only

Alois Hitler was a cobbler turned civil servant; he was described as 'stern, correct, industrious, punctual and clear-headed'.

to his mother's relations. There are many things to suggest that Adolf Hitler's grandfather was not Johann Georg Hiedler, but an unknown one.'

'The ancestors on both sides of the family were peasant people of the district of Waldviertel, highly illiterate and very inbred,' said Vernon.

Alois Hitler was a cobbler. In 1873 he married Anna Glassl, who was fifteen years his senior. She had connections in the civil service and he became a provincial customs officer. After a short time Anna became ill and he began an affair with Franziska 'Fanni' Matzelsberger. In 1880, Anna obtained a legal separation and Alois and Fanni then lived together openly. Six weeks after Anna died in 1883, they married. One of Fanni's first acts as Alois's wife was to banish his second cousin, Klara Pölzl, who had been looking after their two children, from the household.

Fanni died a year later and Alois immediately recalled Klara to Braunau am Inn on the border with Germany, where he then lived. They married three months later.

Heiden said that Alois looked like Hindenburg with a big head, a large handlebar moustache and a heavy chin.

'Alois Hitler has been described as a stern, correct, industrious, punctual, and clear-headed man; in many things, the exact opposite of his son,' said Heiden, while Klara was described as 'a tall, nervous young woman, not as strong as most peasant stock, who ran off to Vienna as a girl to return after ten years (a daring escapade for one in her social status)'.

She had three children in quick succession, who all died before they were three. Born on 20 April 1889, Adolf was her fourth child and the first to live beyond infancy. Consequently she lavished her affection upon him. In return, Adolf, who feared and opposed his father, gave all this affection back to his mother. When she died of breast cancer in 1907, he was prostrate with grief.

EARLY LIFE

As a boy, Adolf was tall, sallow and old for his age, with large melancholy eyes. Vernon found no evidence that he was particularly sickly as a child,

Hitler's mother Klara was a devout Catholic and regularly went to church with her children. She doted on her son Adolf.

though he suffered the usual sore throats and colds. Though in *Mein Kampf* Hitler claimed to have had a serious lung ailment, his family doctor Eduard Bloch said this was not true. He would walk in the mountains, swim in the Danube and read James Fenimore Cooper and Karl May, a German author of American Old West stories. While Hitler portrayed himself as a young tough, he was a quiet, well-mannered boy who kept himself to himself.

Little was known about his early education, beyond his own account. He wanted to be an artist, but his father was determined that he should become another civil servant, causing a perpetual struggle between them. Adolf's mother sided with him and when his father died he went off to Vienna to complete his art education. But he failed his entrance examination to the Academy of Fine Arts. Apart from history and geography, he had neglected his studies at school. This prevented him getting into architectural school.

He was nineteen when his mother died. He then spent three lonely and miserable years in Vienna, living in flophouses and eking out a living by begging, shovelling snow, peddling postcards or working as a hod-carrier or a casual labourer. According to Vernon: 'Here his ideas began to crystallize, his anti-Semitism and anti-Slavism, his anti-ideas of all sorts.'

In 1913, he moved to Munich and earned some sort of a living as a watercolour artist, picture postcard painter, technical draughtsman and occasional house painter. At the outbreak of World War I, he enlisted in the German army with great enthusiasm, performing his duties with distinction and bravery. Vernon listed his military awards – Regimental Diploma for Conspicuous Bravery; Military Cross for Distinguished Service, Third Class; the Black Wounded Badge; and the Iron Cross, First Class.

Wounded, Hitler was sent home to recover. In March 1917, he was back at the front. He was aloof from his comrades, zealous in his duties and very lonely. It was said that throughout the war he never received a letter or a parcel.

The war over and with no home to go to, Hitler returned to Munich. In 1919, he became an espionage agent for the Reichswehr, the provisional

Hitler at school in Lambach at the age of ten; he was far from an outstanding pupil. Teachers considered him quite able but lazy.

national defence force that had just put down the short-lived Bavarian Soviet Republic in Munich. Shortly afterwards he came into contact with Anton Drexler, founder of the German Workers' Party, the forerunner of the Nazi Party.

SECOND-RATE WAITER

Vernon then examined Hitler's appearance and manner from portraits and newsreels and said:

> 'To most non-Nazis Hitler has no particular attraction. He resembles a second-rate waiter. He is a smallish man, slightly under average height. His forehead is slightly receding and his nose somewhat incongruous with the rest of his face. The latter is somewhat soft, his lips thin, and the whole face expressionless. The eyes are a neutral grey which tend to take on the colour of their momentary surroundings. The look tends to be staring or dead and lacking in sparkle. There is an essentially feminine quality about his person which is portrayed particularly in his strikingly well-shaped and expressive hands.'

As to his manner, he 'is essentially awkward and all his movements jerky except perhaps the gestures of his hands. He appears shy and ill-at-ease in company and seems seldom capable of carrying on a conversation. Usually he declaims while his associates listen. He often seems listless and moody. This is in marked contrast to the dramatic energy of his speeches and his skilful play upon the emotions of his vast audiences, every changing mood of which he appears to perceive and turn to his own purposes. At times he is conciliatory, at other times he may burst into violent temper tantrums if his whims are checked in any way.'

DIVINE MISSION

To understand his attitudes to nature, fate and religion, Vernon said it was only necessary to look at the first and last words of *Mein Kampf*. He begins by claiming that fate had chosen Braunau am Inn, on the border of the two German states he sought to unite, as his birthplace and in almost the last paragraph he quotes his own closing speech at his trial in 1924, when he appealed to the goddess of history for vindication. Throughout there were references to eternal nature, providence and destiny.

'Therefore, I believe today I am acting in accordance with the will of the Almighty Creator: by warding off the Jews, I am fighting for the work of the Lord,' Hitler wrote.

'No matter how pagan Hitler's ethical and social ideas may be,' Vernon said, 'they have a quality comparable to religious experience. Moreover, all through his acts and words, both spoken and written, is this extreme exaggeration of his own importance – he truly felt that he was on a divine mission, even to the point of foreseeing a martyr's death.'

Both Catholicism and Protestantism were seen as old religions in Hitler's eyes, which must give way to a new one. Conscience was scorned as a Jewish invention, a blemish like circumcision. However, Hitler obeyed his own inner voice.

'Unless I have the inner incorruptible evidence, this is the solution, I do nothing … I will not act, I will wait no matter what happens,' he said. 'But if the voice speaks, then I know the time has come to act.'

When he was making speeches or walking alone in the mountains, Hitler felt he possessed tremendous strength of will, determination and power. But between times he felt weak and humiliated and was irritable and indecisive. This explained his attitude to education, Vernon said.

'All weakness must be knocked out of the new German youth, they must be indifferent to pain, have no fear of death, must learn the art of self-command; for only in this way can they become creative Godmen,' Rauschning recorded in *Hitler Speaks*.

Hitler had contempt for people or nations that were weak.

'My great political opportunity lies in my deliberate use of power at a time when there are still illusions abroad as to the forces that mould history,' he said.

Hitler respected Britain, which he had faced in the Great War, and had disdain for the weak Indian revolutionaries who wanted to throw off imperial rule. War with Britain had only come about again in 1939 because Hitler was convinced the British could not withstand the strength of the German armed forces.

Those that were not powerful were pitiful. Vernon continued:

'For the masses over whom he has sway he feels only contempt. He compares them to a woman who prefers to submit to the will of someone stronger. He harangues the crowd at night when they are tired and less resistant to the will of another. He uses every psychological trick to break the will of an audience. He makes use of all the conditions which make in the German people for a longing for submission, their anxieties, their feelings of loneliness. He understands his subjects because they are so like himself.'

Closely related to this attitude, and one of the basic elements of the structure of his personality, Vernon said, was Hitler's deep-lying need for aggression, destruction and brutality. Hitler himself said that this was with him in fantasy form in childhood and it was with him in his days in Vienna, according to his friend Reinhold Hanisch, whose recollections were published as *I Was Hitler's Buddy*. Consequently, Hitler was thrilled when World War I broke out.

Vernon wrote:

'Since the war we have seen his adoption of the so-called "communist" methods of dealing with hecklers, the murder of his close friends, his brutality toward the Jews, his destruction of one small nation after another, and his more recent major war against the rest of the world. But this element of his personality is so patent that it hardly needs documenting.'

SEX LIFE

Clearly Hitler's attitude to sex was also pathological. However, Vernon said he did not have access to the sources that would tell him explicitly what was wrong with Hitler's sex life. Hitler's early association with Ernst Röhm, leader of his storm troopers, and other homosexuals sparked gossip, but reliable sources denied that Hitler had any proclivities in that direction. He had no close male friends and Röhm was the only one he addressed with the intimate '*du*'. Since Hitler had had Röhm murdered in the Night of the Long Knives, no one had taken over his role.

The newspapers stressed Hitler's asceticism and his lack of interest in women, but Heiden documented his love affairs. Hanisch, Rauschning and Strasser also mention his attitude to the opposite sex.

Vernon said that:

'As far as can be ascertained, it is completely lacking in respect, even contemptuous, it is opportunistic, and in the actual sexual relationship there is something of a perverse nature along with a peculiar enslavement to the partner of his choice.'

While many women found him fascinating and he enjoyed their company, Vernon noted that every affair was broken off by the lady concerned, not by Hitler. Then there was the tragedy of his affair with his niece Geli Raubal, who Hitler either murdered in a fit of passion or abused so badly that she committed suicide. The daughter of Hitler's half-sister Angela, she lived in Hitler's apartment at the Brown House, the Nazi headquarters in Munich, where she was found dead on 18 September 1931, killed by a bullet from Hitler's pistol. According to Otto Strasser, the public prosecutor wanted to charge Hitler with murder, but the Bavarian Minister of Justice, Wilhelm Gürtner, quashed the case and a verdict of suicide was recorded. Gürtner went on to become Reich Minister of Justice, while the hapless prosecutor fled Germany when Hitler came to power.

In *Mein Kampf* Hitler repeatedly railed against syphilis as if the whole German nation were a vast putrifying hotbed of the loathsome disease.

'Heiden's statement that "there is something wrong" with Hitler's sex life is surely an eloquent understatement,' Vernon concluded.

NEED TO TALK

Plainly Hitler had a need to talk. His frequent speeches lasted between an hour and a half to two hours. In private, he seldom conversed, addressing each individual as if they were a new audience to be harangued. When depressed, he needed to talk to prove his own strength by dominating others. Vernon speculated that from the analytical point of view this may well be interpreted as a compensation for his sexual difficulties.

When it came to music, Wagner was not just Hitler's favourite composer, he was his only composer. At twelve, he was captivated by *Lohengrin*; at nineteen he was championing the merits of Wagner over those of Mozart in Vienna. As Führer he had seen *Die Meistersinger* over a hundred times. He knew all of Wagner's scores, drawing inspiration particularly from *The Ring*, and hearing Wagner's music gave him emotional release. He borrowed many of his attitudes about sex, racial purity, food and drink, and even his saviour complex, from Wagner.

Nuremberg was chosen for the annual Nazi Party Congress because of its association with Wagner. Among Hitler's favourite reading were Wagner's political writings and he borrowed the composer's bombastic style. His vegetarianism and his abstinence from tobacco and alcohol were due to Wagner's influence. This was all the more remarkable among a people known for their love of heavy eating and drinking.

Siegfried awakens Brunhilde in this scene from Wagner's *The Ring*; Hitler was besotted with Wagner's work.

In art, he showed a preoccupation with architecture, old ruins and empty, desolate places, but surrounded himself with military pictures and explicit nudes, while purging German art of modernism. All important buildings and monuments had to be approved by him and needed to conform to his taste for the classic and massive.

UNUSUAL ABILITIES

While uneducated, Vernon found Hitler to be a man of unusual abilities, particularly that of reducing a complicated problem to simple terms.

'It is hardly necessary to document Hitler's ability to understand and make use of the weaknesses of his opponents, his ability to divide them and strike them one by one, his sense of timing so as to strike at the most opportune moment,' he said.

But Hitler did have his limitations. As he became more isolated, he lost contact with what was really going on and based his decisions on incomplete or incorrect data. He also had problems understanding people 'outside the European milieu'.

'He has, consequently, frequently misunderstood both British and American points of view with unhappy results to his own programme of expansion,' said Vernon.

There were other symptoms of maladjustment. He suffered from severe insomnia and when he did sleep he had violent nightmares. At times he had hallucinations and often heard voices on his long, solitary walks.

He had an excessive fear of poisoning, taking extreme precautions with his food, and his bed had to be made up in a specific way. He could not work steadily, but only in explosive outbursts of energy or not at all. Even the smallest decision demanded the greatest effort and he had to work himself up to it. When thwarted, he would have a hysterical tantrum, scolding others in a high-pitched voice, foaming at the mouth and stamping uncontrollably in fury. On several occasions, when he was to make an important speech, he stood in silence before his audience, then walked out, and one international broadcast was inexplicably taken off air. And he threatened to commit suicide if the Nazi Party was destroyed or his plans for the German Reich failed.

SCHIZOID TEMPERAMENT

Vernon also tried to analyse the sources of Hitler's maladjustments.

> 'The schizoid temperament, one such as Hitler's, which combines both a sensitive, shy, and indrawn nature with inhibitions of feeling toward others, and at the same time, in way of compensation, violent aggressiveness, callousness, and brutality, from one point of view of constitutional psychology is usually associated with a particular type of physique.'

But from the photographs available, Vernon found it difficult to judge Hitler's physique accurately.

He referred to the work of German psychiatrist Ernst Kretschmer who believed that there were three main body types. These were the asthenic/leptosomic, which was thin, small and weak; the athletic, which was muscular and large-boned; and the pyknic, which was stocky and fat. Each of these body types was associated with certain personality traits and, in a more extreme form, psychopathologies. Vernon thought that Hitler probably fell into the athletic, verging on the pyknic.

'This would place him in the schizophrenic group of temperaments,' he said.

Vernon also referred to the system developed by American psychologist William Herbert Sheldon, classifying Hitler as a '443' with a considerable degree of gynandromorphism – that is, an essentially masculine body but one also showing feminine characteristics.

SOCIAL MILIEU

Then there was the social milieu he grew up in. In a strongly patriarchal society, his father was particularly aggressive and brutal towards his son.

'This would produce an individual both very submissive to authority and at the same time boiling over with rebellion to it,' said Vernon.

Hitler also exhibited an extreme attachment to his mother.

'If, as seems likely, he has never outgrown this, there might be a protest in his nature against this enslavement, which in turn might give rise to a deep unconscious hatred, a possible source of frightful unconscious rage.'

Vernon again noted that Hitler often used the word 'motherland' when referring to Germany. He also remarked: 'Hitler's hatred of meat and love of sweets is said to be often found in cases harbouring unconscious hate of the mother.'

Hitler's failure as an artist, his loneliness and poverty in Vienna and his failure to rise higher than the rank of corporal in his beloved army 'must have stimulated to the highest degree whatever original tendency there was toward brutality and destructiveness'.

ANTI-SEMITISM

Hitler claimed to have been anti-Semitic from an early age, avoiding the only Jewish boy at school. This was not uncommon in rural areas. But his deep-rooted hatred of Jews was inflamed by violent anti-Semitic literature. Vernon pointed out that Hitler was not an uncommon Jewish name and that he was teased about his Jewish appearance in Vienna. There were also rumours about his father's parentage. Many of the people who helped him, gave him food and bought his paintings were Jews.

'To have to accept kindnesses from people he disliked would not add to his love of them,' said Vernon. 'But there must be more to it than this for Hitler's anti-Semitism is bound up with his morbid concern with syphilis and phobia over contamination of the blood of the German race.'

Vernon also noted: 'His rejection of the Jew may also stem from the rejection within himself of the passive gentle elements which are prominent in Hebrew-Christian thought.'

According to Vernon, syphilophobia often had its roots in the childhood discovery of the nature of sexual congress between the parents.

'Such a discovery by the child Adolf may well have laid the basis of a syphilophobia which some adventure with a Jewish prostitute in Vienna fanned to a full flame,' Vernon said, though he admitted this was only conjecture, but 'fits known psychological facts'.

VERNON'S INTERPRETATION

Vernon then gave 'one possible psychological interpretation'.

> 'Hitler's personality structure, though falling within the normal range, may now be described as of the paranoid type with delusions of persecution and of grandeur. This stems from a sado-masochistic split in his personality. Integral with these alternating and opposed elements in his personality are his fear of infection, the identification of the Jews as the source of that infection, and some derangement of the sexual function which makes his relations to the opposite sex abnormal in nature.'

According to Vernon, the key to Hitler's personality lay in his troubled childhood relations with his parents.

> 'The drama and tragedy of Hitler's life are the projection onto the world of his own inner conflicts and his attempts to solve them. The split in Hitler's personality seems clearly to be due to his identification both with his mother, whom he passionately loved, and with his father, whom he hated and feared. This dual and contradictory identification (the one is gentle, passive, feminine; the other brutal, aggressive, masculine) results – whenever Hitler is playing the aggressive role – also in a deep hatred and contempt for his mother and love and admiration for his father. This inner conflict is projected into the world where Germany comes to represent the mother, and the Jew and – for a time – the Austrian State, the father. Just as the father is the cause of his mixed blood, the source of his domination and punishment, and of the restrictions on his own artistic development; just as in the childish interpretation of sexual congress the father attacks, strangles, and infects the mother; so the Jew, international Jewish capital, etc., encircle and restrict Germany, threaten and attack her and infect her with impurities of blood. Out of the hatred of the father and love of the mother came the desire to save her. So Hitler becomes the saviour of Germany, who cleanses her of infection,

destroys her enemies, breaks their encirclement, removes every restriction upon her so that she may expand into new living space, uncramped and unthrottled. At the same time, Hitler is cleansing himself, defending himself, casting off paternal domination and restriction.'

Not only was his father feared but he was a source of jealousy for he possessed, at least in part, Hitler's beloved mother. So he must be destroyed to permit Hitler's complete possession of her. The destruction of his father was achieved symbolically by the destruction of the Austrian state and complete domination and possession of the mother through gathering all Germans into a common Reich.

'But the mother is not only loved but hated. For she is weak, besides he is enslaved to her affections and she reminds him all too much, in his role as dominant father, of his own gentle sensitive nature. So, though he depends on the German people for his position of dominance, he despises and hates them, he dominates them and, because he fears his very love of them, he leads them into the destructiveness of war where multitudes of them are destroyed. Besides, the Jewish element in his father's identification permits him to use all the so-called "Jewish" tricks of deceit, lying, violence, and sudden attack both to subject the German people as well as their foes.'

Even the complete domination of the German people had its problems psychologically.

'To be dominant, aggressive, brutal is to arouse the violent protest of the other side of his nature. Only severe anxiety can come from this; nightmares and sleepless nights result. But fear is assuaged by the fiction of the demands of Fate, of Destiny, of the Folk-Soul of the German people.'

But an end would come, said Vernon.

'The denouement of the drama approaches at every aggressive step. The fiction of the command of Fate only holds as long as there is success – greater and greater success to assuage the mounting feelings of anxiety and guilt. Aggression, therefore, has a limit; it cannot go beyond the highest point of success. When that is reached, the personality may collapse under the flood of its own guilt feelings. (That Hitler is partly conscious of this we know from his own threats of suicide and references to dying for the German people.) It is, therefore, quite possible that Hitler will do away with himself at whatever moment German defeat becomes sufficient enough to destroy the fiction of Fate which has shielded him from the violence of his own guilt. He may then turn upon himself the destructiveness which so long has been channelled toward his people and their neighbours.'

December 1941 and Hitler launches into his diatribe against Roosevelt in the Reichstag as Germany declares war on the USA.

CHAPTER 3
Analysing Adolf

In 1938, the administration of President Franklin Delano Roosevelt asked Professor Henry A. Murray, MD, of the Harvard Psychological Clinic to investigate the psyche of Hitler. One of the early champions of psychoanalysis in the United States, Murray was inspired by Carl Jung, an early associate of Freud, and was a founder of the Boston Psychoanalytic Society. Also a leading authority on the life and work of Herman Melville, he once gave Freud a copy of *Moby Dick* and reported that the father of psychoanalysis promptly proclaimed that 'the whale was a father figure'.

Murray did not complete his investigation until October 1943, after he was recruited by the OSS, the forerunner of the Central Intelligence Agency (CIA), to apply his knowledge of psychology in selecting undercover agents. His typewritten report, *Analysis of the Personality of Adolf Hitler with Predictions of His Future Behavior and Suggestions for Dealing with Him Now and After Germany's Surrender*, was then compiled for the OSS. In it, he said:

> 'Hitler's unprecedented appeal, the elevation of this to the status of a demigod, can be explained only on the hypothesis that he and his ideology have almost exactly met the needs, longings, and sentiments of the majority of Germans.'

He also said that he had based his analysis on data supplied by the OSS, Hitler's book *Mein Kampf*, the collection of his speeches titled *My New*

Order, Hitler: A Biography by Konrad Heiden and *Germany Possessed* by Dr H.G. Baynes, another Jungian, who based his work on Rauschning's records of conversations with Hitler and Rauschning's own *Voice of Destruction*, the US edition of *Hitler Speaks*. He also included Vernon's paper as an introduction.

The report talked of Hitler's megalomania – or 'delusions of omnipotence' – which had come about because countervailing forces, such as affection, conscience, self-criticism or humour within him were so weak. As a result Hitler had 'succeeded in getting a large proportion of the German people to believe that he is superior: (i) that he had been divinely appointed to lead them to power and glory, and (ii) that he is *never wrong* and hence must be followed with blind obedience, come what may'.

MAN OF CONTRADICTIONS

Murray drew attention to the fact that Hitler lauded the very qualities he did not himself possess. He admired brute strength and had a contempt for weakness, even though Murray maintained he was a frail and sickly child, never did any manual work or engaged in athletics and was turned down as unfit by the Austrian army. He was also afraid of his father and was obsequiously subservient to his superior officers in the German army. At the end of the war, he broke down with a war neurosis, hysterical blindness.

'Even lately, in all his glory,' said Murray, 'he suffers from frequent emotional collapses in which he yells and weeps. He had nightmares from a bad conscience; and he had long spells when energy, confidence and the power of decision abandon him. Sexually he is a full-fledged masochist.'

While Hitler admired 'pure noble German blood' and 'never ceased expressing his contempt of the lower classes', he came from 'illiterate peasant stock derived from a mixture of races, no pure Germans among them. His father was illegitimate, was married three times, and is said to have been conspicuous for sexual promiscuity. Hitler's mother was a domestic servant.'

Then there was his aversion to Jews.

'It is said that Hitler's father's father was a Jew, and it is certain that his godfather was a Jew; and that one of his sisters managed a restaurant for Jewish students in Vienna and another was, for a time, the mistress of a Jew. Hitler's appearance, when he wore a long beard during his outcast Vienna days, was said to be very Jewish. Of these facts he is evidently ashamed. Unlike Napoleon, he has rejected all his relations.'

Murray said he had a partial explanation for Hitler's complex about impurity of blood:

'As a boy of twelve, Hitler was caught engaging in some sexual experiment with a little girl; and later he seems to have developed a syphilophobia [a fear of catching syphilis] with a diffuse fear of contamination of the blood through contact with a woman. It is almost certain that this irrational dread was partly due to the association in his mind of sexuality and excretion. He thought of sexual relations as something exceedingly filthy.'

Hitler was an advocate of fertility as the family was the breeding ground of warriors, yet Hitler himself was impotent, Murray maintained.

'He is unmarried and his old acquaintances say that he is incapable of consummating the sexual act in a normal fashion. This infirmity we must recognize as an instigation to exorbitant cravings for superiority. Unable to demonstrate male power before a woman, he is impelled to compensate by exhibiting unsurpassed power before men in the world at large.'

ORATORY

Unable to change his origins or his sexual potency, and unwilling to develop himself physically as Mussolini had, he was hell-bent on making himself the most powerful man in the world by his oratory.

Murray wrote:

'Hitler speaking before a large audience is a man possessed, comparable to a primitive medicine man, or shaman. He is the incarnation of the crowd's unspoken needs and cravings; and in this sense he has been created, and to a large extent invented, by the people of Germany.'

Hitler compared the masses to a woman who must be 'courted with the arts and skills known to passion only; and it is not unlikely that the emotional sources of his orgiastic speeches were childhood tantrums by which he successfully appealed to his ever-indulgent mother'.

But Murray conceded that the will to power and the craving for superiority did not account for the whole of Hitler's psychology. There was also an 'immeasurable hatred' that constantly sought out an object on which he could vent his pent-up wrath.

'This can be traced back with relative certainty to experiences of insult, humiliation and wounded pride in childhood,' Murray said.

His hypothesis was that 'as a boy Hitler was severely shocked (as it were, blinded) by witnessing sexual intercourse between his parents, and his reaction to this trauma was to swear revenge, to dream of himself re-establishing the lost glory of his mother by overcoming and humiliating his father.'

As a frail child that was impossible, so the impulse was repressed, only to emerge much later when he witnessed the subjugation and humiliation of his 'motherland' – as he unusually called Germany – in 1918. The impulse for revenge was then released through a short period of shock and hysterical blindness. Murray believed that his hypothesis explained why Hitler exhibited no ambitious drive from the age of thirteen, when his father died, to the age of twenty-nine when a new danger threatened his motherland. In *Mein Kampf*, Hitler repeatedly referred to Germany as a beloved woman and explained why he was so devoted to her rehabilitation.

OEDIPUS COMPLEX

According to Murray, in Hitler the ordinary Oedipus complex – love of mother, hate of father – was overwritten by another pattern: his

New technology, radio, meant Hitler could reach a vast audience; he could rant to his heart's content and know he was being listened to.

admiration, envy and emulation of his father's masculine power and a contempt of his mother's submissiveness and weakness. This vast reservoir of resentment and revenge gave him a homicidal compulsion towards scapegoating and war.

But Murray did not consider Hitler a 'healthy amoral brute' like Göring and other associates.

'Every new act of unusual cruelty, such as the purge of 1934, has been followed by a period of anxiety and depletion, agitated dejection and nightmares, which can be interpreted only as the unconscious operation of a bad conscience.'

Despite boasting that he had transcended Good and Evil, Hitler wanted nothing so much as to arrive at the state where he could commit crimes without feeling guilt. Murray also noted that Hitler never had any close personal friends.

'He is entirely incapable of normal human relationships. This is due, in part, to the cessation in early life of sexual development,' said Murray.

Having set out on a life of crime, Hitler could not reverse his course without admitting that he was wrong. Consequently, as his unconscious guilt grew, he was forced to commit even more barbarous acts of aggression which, if successful, would prove that he was right in the first place.

He also projected things that he could condemn in himself on to other people who were said to be treacherous, lying, corrupt and warmongering. All his own faults were blamed on his political opponents.

Murray said that Hitler, at one time or another, 'exhibited all the classical symptoms of paranoid schizophrenia: hypersensitivity, panics of anxiety, irrational jealousy, delusions of persecution, delusions of omnipotence and messiahship'. He went on to wonder how Hitler 'escaped confinement as a dangerous psychopath'.

TEARS AND SELF-PITY

In the face of opposition, Hitler resorted to emotional outbursts, tantrums of rage, accusations and indignation, ending in tears and self-pity. These were succeeded by periods of inertia, exhaustion, melancholy and indecisiveness, sometimes accompanied by hours of dejection and nightmares. Then, in recuperation, he would appear confident

Hitler addresses a mass rally of the SA in Dortmund, 1933. You can easily imagine the feeling of power.

and resolute, taking the decision to counterattack with great force and ruthlessness. The entire cycle could take a single day, or weeks. This had worked in his favour until, on the Russian front, his counterattacks failed, often disastrously.

'There is no structure for defence in Hitler's personality,' said Murray. 'He can only strike when inflated with confidence or collapse when confidence abandons him.'

And he predicted that Hitler's periods of collapse would increase in intensity, frequency and duration, while his confidence and power of retaliation decreased.

'A point to be remembered about Hitler,' wrote Murray, 'is that he started his career at scratch, a nonentity with nothing to lose, and he selected a fanatical path for himself which requires as an ending complete success (omnipotence) or utter failure (death).'

As he was not personally doing the fighting, he could collapse in private at his retreat at Berchtesgaden, where he could recuperate, then come back with an ever more desperate plan to destroy the enemy.

'There is a powerful compulsion in him to sacrifice himself and all of Germany to the revengeful annihilation of Western culture, to die, dragging all of Europe with him into the abyss,' Murray said. 'This he would feel was the last resource of an insulted and unendurable existence.'

Murray surmised that Hitler's youthful enthusiasm for painting was because it was the one thing he excelled at in school. It also provided 'an acceptable outlet for a destructive soiling tendency repressed in infancy'. This was balanced with the constructiveness shown in his love of architecture. While he enjoyed painting ruined temples – much as he later enjoyed ruined cities – he also liked painting huge castles, and later designing grandiose buildings for the Third Reich.

Hitler was not entirely devoted to destruction, Murray said. 'In his nature there is a deep valid strain of creativeness (lacking, to be sure, the necessary talent). In the allegory of his own life, he was the author and leading actor of a great drama.'

An analysis of the metaphors used in *Mein Kampf* led Murray to identify in Hitler 'a primitive excretory soiling tendency', 'a passive masochistic tendency', 'an unconscious need for punishment' and 'repressed (or as some claim overt) homosexuality'. To support these conjectures, he cited Hitler's femininity; his identification with his mother; his subservience to superior officers; and his attraction to Sturmabteilung (SA) leader Ernst Röhm, who died with other Nazi homosexuals on the Night of the Long Knives. Hitler's nightmares were 'very suggestive of homosexual panic', Murray said. So were some of Hitler's interpretations of human nature, such as when he said that people 'want someone to frighten them and make them shudderingly submissive'. He made repeated assertions that he intended, like Roman dictator Lucius Cornelius Sulla, 'to abdicate power (after an orgy of conquest with full catharsis of his hate) and live quietly by himself, painting and designing buildings'. There were also his recurrent suicide threats.

EGOCENTRIC CRAVINGS

Murray claimed that Hitler was 'ideocentric', since he was clearly devoted to the Prussian militarism ideal for Germany. He could also be seen as 'sociocentric', as he had a plan in which the majority of Germans would supposedly benefit. But these characteristics were clearly secondary to his egocentric craving for fame and immortality.

His intensive affection for the Reich – 'perhaps felt to this extent only by a nationalist born outside its boundaries' – had won him the support of the people, satisfying his craving for power. It also gave him a sense of vocation and provided, in his own mind at least, moral justification for numerous illegal acts. And it kept him relatively sane as it brought him into contact with like-minded men in the Nazi Party and spared him the consequences of psychological isolation.

Why, when living as an outcast in Vienna, did Hitler not become a communist? Murray asked. The answer was that while his father had started as a peasant, he had worked his way up into the lower middle classes. Both parents respected their social superiors. Too weak for construction work, he had been cut off from the labouring classes in Vienna and, unable to hold down a job, he had little opportunity to join a trade union.

A nationalist from the age of twelve, Hitler saw the political struggle as that between nations, rather than between classes. He favoured the hierarchical principle 'the fittest should rule', rather than the distribution of power among the masses. He was a militarist, not a materialist, and lacked sympathy for the underdog. By nature, he was a bully.

HITLER'S ABILITIES

Murray listed Hitler's abilities and effective traits – he could:

1. Express with passion the deepest needs and longings of the people
2. Appeal to the most primitive as well as to the most ideal tendencies in men
3. Simplify complex problems and arrive at the quickest solution
4. Use metaphor and draw on traditional imagery and myth in speaking and writing
5. Evoke the sympathy and protectiveness of the German people *and possessed*:
6. Complete dedication to his mission, abundant self-confidence and stubborn adherence to a few principles
7. Mastery of political organization
8. Tactical genius and precise timing
9. Mastery of the art of propaganda.

SCAPEGOATS

Murray also examined the origins of Hitler's anti-Semitism, which was, of course, common in Germany at the time. His personal frustrations required a scapegoat – and, traditionally, Jews did not fight back. He could also project on to Jews his sensitivity, weakness, timidity and masochism.

After Germany's defeat in World War I, the German people also needed a scapegoat, so picking on the Jews was a matter of political strategy. It was easy to turn his storm troopers on them. Being non-militaristic, they were unlikely to impede his progress and picking on them lost him no sizable support. They were associated with many of his pet antipathies – business, materialism, democracy, capitalism,

The offices of the virulently anti-Semitic paper *Der Stürmer* in Danzig –
the poster in the window says, 'The Jews are our misfortune'.

communism. Some were very rich and he needed some excuse for dispossessing them.

Murray noted that Hitler had a weak character; his great strength came from his emotional complexity. While he could not force himself to stick to a routine of work, he could apply himself when lifted on a wave of passion.

While Hitler 'clearly belongs to the sensational company of history-making hysterics', he had a large measure of control over his complexes, using his emotional outbursts to get his own way. As a borderline schizophrenic, the possibility of a complete mental breakdown was not remote. However, his paranoia protected him because it was effective in rousing the forces of a minor party or a defeated nation. He used his delusions of persecution to create a vivid and exaggerated word-picture of the crimes and treacherous evils of powerful opponents. The concomitant delusions of grandeur were useful to persuade followers of their innate superiority and of the glorious destiny that awaited them.

Their enemies had used dastardly tactics against them in the past, so they were justified in using any means to destroy them. What's more, their enemies could be blamed for any frustration or reverse. In this way Hitler exploited his own paranoid tendencies and retained some control over them, avoiding insanity by using them to achieve his own ends.

HITLER'S PRINCIPLES OF POLITICAL ACTION

Murray also listed the guiding principles of Hitler's political philosophy:

1. Success depended on winning the support of the masses.
2. The leader of a new movement must appeal to youth.
3. The masses needed a sustaining ideology and the leader must provide one.
4. People do not act if their emotions are not aroused.
5. Artistry and drama were needed at political rallies and meetings.
6. The leader must be the creator of ideas and plans.

7. Success justifies any means.
8. A new movement cannot triumph with the elective use of terroristic methods.

FUTURE BEHAVIOUR

After examining Hitler's character Murray made predictions about his future behaviour. He had already noted that his mental powers had deteriorated since November 1942, when the British defeated Erwin Rommel at the Battle of El Alamein, Allied troops landed in Morocco and Algeria and the German Sixth Army had been surrounded at Stalingrad.

If his mental condition deteriorated much further, the German General Staff might imprison him or even hand him over to the Allies. Murray thought this unlikely because of the widespread reverence for him.

Hitler might be shot by some disaffected German, something he had been afraid of for years. But this too Murray thought unlikely as Germans were not inclined to shoot their leaders and Hitler was protected like never before.

Hitler might arrange to have himself assassinated. Death at the hands of a trusted follower would complete the hero myth – as in the epic German poem *The Nibelungenlied*, upon which Wagner had based his *Ring* cycle, where Siegfried was stabbed in the back by Hagen; or when Julius Caesar was stabbed by Brutus; or Christ was betrayed by Judas. This might inspire his troops to new acts of fanaticism and his legend would endure. If he could arrange for a Jew to kill him, the Germans might massacre every remaining Jew in Germany, indulging Hitler's insatiable lust for revenge.

He might get himself killed by leading his men into battle. It would ensure his immortality – one of Hitler's favourite poses was Siegfried leading the Aryan hosts against Bolshevism and the Slavs. This would be very undesirable from the Allied point of view as it might inspire his followers to fight on fanatically to the bitter end.

A better outcome would be if Hitler went insane, which Murray considered not unlikely. Even if this was hidden from the German people,

Pre-Holocaust German propaganda: Hitler did not invent anti-Semitism but he exploited it to the full to spread fear and gain power.

rumours would spread, damaging morale and the legend of the hero would be severely impaired.

He might commit suicide, as he had often threatened to do before when thwarted. Murray assumed that if he chose that course, he would wait until the last moment and do it in the most dramatic way possible. He envisaged Hitler retiring to the Berghof, his mountain retreat at Berchtesgaden, then blowing up the mountain with dynamite when troops approached. Or turning the house into a funeral pyre and throwing himself on to it, in a scenario worthy of Wagner's *Götterdämmerung*. Or he might throw himself off the parapet or shoot himself with a silver bullet.

He might die of natural causes or seek refuge in a neutral country. This was not likely, though some associates might drug him and put him on a plane to Switzerland, where he might be persuaded to write his long-promised bible for the German folk. But again this would damage his hero-image.

Last and possibly the least likely was that he would fall into the hands of an Allied army.

HITLER IN CAPTIVITY

Murray then considered what they should do with Hitler if they did capture him. Any of the conventional punishments – a trial followed by execution, life imprisonment or exile – might help resurrect and perpetuate the Hitler legend. Rather, after the trial and execution of the other Nazi leaders, Hitler should be declared insane and committed to an asylum – Murray suggested St Elizabeths in Washington, DC – where the world should know he was being well treated, with a committee of psychiatrists and psychologists visiting him regularly.

However, he should be filmed secretly, showing his fits and tirades. In them he would naturally condemn everyone in the world, including the German people. The footage should be exhibited regularly so that people could see how unbalanced he was. He could also be filmed performing badly at simple tests. That way, people would tire of him in a year or so.

Hitler's case should be presented to the world as a lesson, telling people, 'This is what happens to crack-brain fanatics who try to dominate the world.' It could also serve as a deterrent to others with fantasies of world domination.

Another deterrent might be a case study in book form that could also contribute to the science of psychiatry.

ENDING THE WAR

To help bring the war to a conclusion, the Allies should either aim to accelerate Hitler's mental deterioration and drive him insane, or try to prevent him from ending his life dramatically and tragically, thereby perpetuating his legend.

Murray did not enumerate the techniques available to give Hitler a nervous breakdown as none could be so effective as repeated military setbacks. Consequently, the Allies should concentrate on deterring Hitler from arranging a hero's or a martyr's death for himself. To do that, they should make him believe that the immortality of his legend would not suffer if he fell into Allied hands.

Murray's plan was to flood Germany with propaganda leaflets and broadcasts, quoting Hess, Rauschning, Strasser and other Nazis in Britain and North America, saying that Hitler could not be trusted and was planning, treacherously, to leave the German people to their fate by getting himself killed. He cared nothing for the German people, only for his own glory. He was no better than a captain deserting a sinking ship. It was an easy way out, a cowardly betrayal.

If hundreds of such pamphlets – with cartoons depicting him rushing forward in a ludicrous charge on the Russian front over the bodies of noble Germans who had died for his glory – were dropped over Berchtesgaden, the chances were that Hitler would see them. He was very susceptible to ridicule. If his suicide or death in battle was made suitably grotesque and ridiculous it might deter him. At the very least, prediction would spoil its dramatic effect.

Murray suggested that Germany should also be flooded with propaganda, saying that all the Nazi leaders who had led the country into such a disastrous war were to be executed, except Hitler. He was to be exiled to St Helena. As a fan of Napoleon, this would appeal to him. He would, no doubt, picture himself painting landscapes, writing his

Germanic bible and plotting an even greater German revolution to be carried out in his name, perhaps in thirty years' time. Only later would he discover that this was a trick.

THE GERMAN PEOPLE

Murray also had some suggestions on how the German people should be treated. First their faith in Hitler must be shaken. Leaflets should be printed containing the name, rank and regiment of German soldiers recently taken prisoner as the Gestapo could hardly prevent anxious parents picking them up. They should carry news of the latest disasters from the front and quotes from prisoners saying that they were happy they were going to prison camps in the United States, the 'land of the free', while the readers were stuck in a Germany that was run by the Gestapo. As a certain reverence was still attached to Hitler's name, he should be referred to as the False Prophet or the False Messiah and later as the Amateur Strategist, Corporal Satan or World Criminal Number One.

Germans liked to look up to God, the state or the Führer, so higher symbols should be substituted. The Allies should be referred to as the World Federation, its armies as the World Army. Set against the False Prophet, propagandists should speak of the World Conscience. One suggestion for a leaflet was to pose the questions: 'Who has seduced the German people from their true path? Who has turned their hearts against the Conscience of the World? Who is responsible this time for Germany's encirclement by the World Army?'

Quotations from the unexpurgated first edition of *Mein Kampf* showing Hitler's contempt for the masses should be included. Hitler's fate should be compared with that of Mussolini, depicting it as the Decline and Fall of the Unholy Alliance. Germans believed in predestination, Murray thought, so the defeat of the False Prophet should be considered a foregone conclusion. Some messages should come from the 'Voice of History'.

Propagandists should play on Hitler's mental decline. For example: 'Now that Mussolini has collapsed and Hitler is in the hands of mental specialists, what has become of the Spirit of Fascism?' or 'Do you still believe that a man whose sanity has been completely undermined by Guilt can lead the German people to victory against the world?'

Play should also be made on Germany's alliance with Japan. For example: 'The Nazis and their blood-brothers, the Japanese, have both demonstrated their willingness to die for Satan – this summer one million of them have thrown away their lives in a futile attempt to destroy civilization.'

Other propaganda material should be taken from the anti-Nazi 'White Rose' manifesto. It was sixth in a series of leaflets produced between July 1942 and February 1943 by students of the University of Munich and their philosophy professor. Six leading members of the group were arrested by the Gestapo, convicted of treason and beheaded. Others were sent to the front as punishment. The leaflet was smuggled out of Germany. Retitled 'The Manifesto of the Munich Students', millions of copies were dropped over Germany by the RAF.

Murray considered that it was psychologically important that Hitler, or whoever was then the leader of the Nazi Party, should be forced to sign a peace treaty. The terms should be severe, but could be made more lenient when a representative government was installed. Then, in future, dictators would be associated with the humiliation of unconditional surrender, while the democratic government would be credited with securing milder terms.

A World Court should be set up with at least one Swiss and one Swedish member, who should immediately publish a list of war criminals, while neutral countries should be warned that no one on the list should be given sanctuary. The Allies should be prepared to invade any country that harboured a war criminal.

Murray recommended that war criminals be tried quickly and that the trials should not be allowed to drag on for months as it would give the impression of moral weakness and incompetence. A simple book should then be published in German, explaining international law and the nature of the crimes committed by the Nazis. (The Nuremberg Trials lasted over ten months and the transcripts run to over 240,000 pages.)

That much blood would be spilt in the final overthrow of the Nazi regime, Murray considered 'a fitting Nemesis'. The Allies would find the

German people profoundly humiliated, resentful, disenchanted, dejected, morose, despairing of the future and there would be a wave of crime and suicide. He went on to outline ways to counter that.

THE MANIFESTO OF THE MUNICH STUDENTS

The German people stand aghast before the destruction of the men of Stalingrad. 330,000 German men have been irresponsibly and uselessly hounded to their death by the brilliant strategy of the World-War-Corporal. Führer, we thank you.

Students, our people are in ferment. Are we going to continue to entrust an amateur with the fate of our Armies? Are we going to sacrifice the remainder of German youth to the lowest power instincts of a Party clique? Never!

The day of reckoning has come, the reckoning of our German youth with the most detestable tyranny which our people has ever had to suffer. In the name of the whole German nation we demand from the state of Adolf Hitler the restitution of personal freedom, that most precious possession of the Germans, out of which we have been cheated.

We have grown up in a state of brutal oppression of all free expression of opinion. The Hitler Youth, the S.A. and the S.S. have tried to regiment, revolutionize and stun us during the most impressionable years of youth. *Weltanschauliche Schulung* [political training] was the term used for the contemptible method of killing the development of individual thought and judgment in a mass of platitudes. In a most devilish and stupid manner future Party chiefs are turned, in *Ordensburgen* [Party Schools] into godless, shameless and irresponsible exploiters and murderers, into blind stupid followers of a leader. It would suit the Party bosses if we, the young intellectuals were to become their willing tools. Soldiers who have seen active fighting are ordered about like schoolboys by student Leaders and *Gauleiter* candidates who have never seen the front. *Gauleiters* attack the honour of girl students by means of filthy jokes. German girl students at Munich University have given a dignified answer to these attacks on their honour, German students have made a stand on behalf of their girl colleagues. That is a beginning of a fight for our free self-determination, without which spiritual values cannot be created. We thank the brave students of either sex who have set such an excellent example.

Monument at the University of Munich to the members of the White Rose movement which opposed Nazism.

We have only one duty; to fight against the Party. Leave the Party organizations which take from us the right of political expression! Boycott the lectures of the Party professors! We are concerned with true learning and real freedom of thought! No threats can frighten us, not even the closing of our universities! For each one of us it is a fight for our future, our freedom and honour in a nation conscious of its moral responsibility!

Freedom and Honour! Hitler and his confederates have for the past ten years used, abused and twisted these two beautiful German words until they have become loathsome. They have thrown the highest ideals of a nation into the gutter! What they mean by freedom and honour they have shown only too well in ten years of destruction of all personal freedom, all freedom

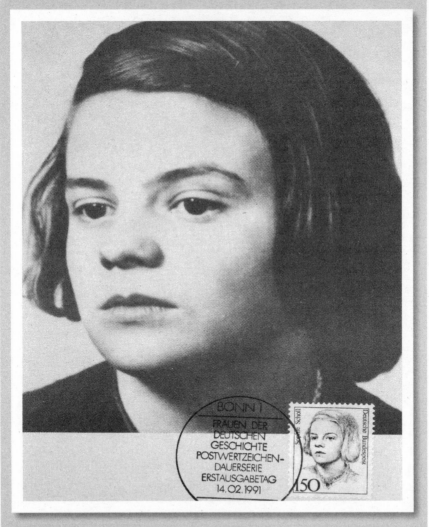

Sophie Scholl, who was convicted of high treason along with her brother Hans and guillotined by the Nazis.

of thought and all moral principles of the German people. The eyes of even the most stupid German have been opened by the terrible bloodbath in which they endeavour to drown all Europe in the name of freedom and honour of the German nation. The German name will remain for ever dishonoured if German youth does not at last arise, revenge and atone, destroy its tormentors and help build up a new spiritual concept of Europe.

CHAPTER 4

Hitler's Personality

After Murray had summarized Vernon's paper he moved on to a 'Detailed Analysis of Hitler's Personality', which was written especially for psychologists and psychiatrists.

This was followed by a 'Statement of the Problem', which was essentially: How, in little over twenty years, could a 'common bum' become 'the most powerful and successful individual on earth, on the one hand, the most worshipped, on the other, the most despised?'

Murray said that this unemployed nonentity had succeeded in becoming a demigod with unlimited power. In the eyes of many German people, he could do no wrong. He was the saviour of his nation, the conqueror of Europe, the divinely appointed prophet of the new era. There was a Hitler Strasse or a Hitler Platz in every town, 'Heil Hitler' was the conventional greeting among acquaintances and his picture was prominently displayed in every public building, railway station and millions of homes. His autobiography was accepted as the bible of a revolutionary folk religion and he was even compared to Christ.

Murray gave another rundown on Hitler's intellectual and physical deficiencies. Frail as a child, he never laboured in the fields or played rough games.

'Discouraged after one attempt to ride a horse, in the last twenty years his exercise has been limited to short walks,' said Murray. He was sexually inadequate and overly feminine.

Examining his medical and psychiatric history, Murray said that Hitler suffered from nervous gastritis, or indigestion, for many years – concluding that this was probably a psychosomatic syndrome, 'part and parcel of his general neuroticism'.

'A German psychiatrist who examined Hitler's medical record in World War I has reported that the diagnosis of his condition was hysterical blindness. In other words, he did not suffer from mustard gas poisoning, as publicly stated, but from a war neurosis. It has also been said that he was not only blind but dumb, and (according to one informant) deaf.'

Later Hitler had a benign polyp removed from his vocal chords, but he remained convinced he had cancer.

His temper tantrums had increased in intensity and frequency in the previous ten years. 'A typical seizure consists of (1) pacing, shouting, cursing, blaming, accusations of treachery and betrayal; (2) weeping and exhibitions of self-pity; and (3) falling on the floor, foaming at the mouth, biting the carpet.'

Murray said that Hitler had some control over these 'epileptiform attacks', using them to get his own way with his close associates.

'Hitler also suffers from agitated depressions, affrighting nightmares, hypochondriacal states in which he fears he will be poisoned or die from cancer of the stomach,' Murray said.

MAN OF PARTS

Despite his utterly insignificant appearance, for ten years the German people had been gazing at Hitler spellbound. Although his eyes were usually staring and dead, impersonal and unseeing, when he fixed someone with an unwavering gaze they were said to be hypnotic. Behind the habitual vacancy of expression some discerned an intense flame of passionate dedication.

While he used his expressive hands effectively when in front of an audience, his handshake was loose and palms clammy. Along with soft features and sallow cheeks, these were hardly evidence of an Iron Man.

Hitler charms Wallis Simpson and the Duke of Windsor in 1937. Foreigners who visited Germany in the 1930s were often impressed.

Murray noted that he played many parts. There was the expressionless Hitler who stood like a dummy with an upraised hand at the front of a motorcade that made its way past serried ranks of cheering adherents. There was the embarrassed Hitler, ill at ease in the presence of a stranger, a great general, an aristocrat or the king of Italy. There was the gracious Hitler, the seemingly modest and good-natured Austrian, welcoming admirers to the Berghof, and the sentimental Hitler, weeping over a dead canary.

On top of all this came the tactical Hitler who made a daring decision at the right moment; the mystical Hitler who promised a thousand years of triumph for the German folk; the possessed Hitler, shrieking with fury as he exhorted the masses; the hysterical Hitler, who shook with terror when awaking from nightmares and rolled on the carpet in a tantrum; the apathetic Hitler, who was indecisive and could barely rouse himself to action; and the soapbox Hitler who went off on a long tirade even though he was addressing a single individual.

PAST HISTORY

Murray then took a detailed look at Hitler's 'Past History'. This began with a Chronology, followed by a chapter on his Childhood and Adolescence, giving a portrait of his mother and father, Hitler's relations with them and his siblings and his boyhood activities and interests. Murray drew on an inquiry ordered by Austrian chancellor Engelbert Dollfuss – who was assassinated by the Nazis in 1934 even though he was a Fascist dictator who had abolished parliament – along with the accounts of Rauschning, Heiden and Hanisch, and *Mein Kampf* and *My New Order*. Again Murray explored Hitler's Oedipus complex and he noted that Hitler had hung a portrait of his father above the desk in his study at Berchtesgaden. In the Berghof's rooms there were likenesses of only three other men – Frederick the Great, Benito Mussolini and the Prussian German Karl von Moltke, who had been instrumental in defeating Denmark in 1864, Austria in 1866 and France in 1871. Nowhere was there a picture of his mother.

Hitler's father was a smoker, a drinker and a lecher and while Hitler was famously abstemious in later life, as a boy he used to pick up cigar butts and smoke them. During his early days in Munich, he drank beer and wine, and latterly showed some interest in women.

**Engelbert Dollfuss lies in state in Austria's Chancellery. He was
assassinated by Nazi sympathizers in 1934.**

'There can be no doubt then that Hitler greatly envied and admired the power and authority of his father,' said Murray, 'and although he hated him as the tyrant who opposed and frustrated him personally, he looked on him with awe and admiration, desiring to be as he was.'

In *Mein Kampf*, Hitler said of his father: 'Unconsciously he had sown seeds for the future which neither he nor I would have grasped at that time.'

From then on Hitler would only take notice of ruthlessly dominating men and if they opposed him he would hate and respect them simultaneously.

Of course, Hitler's many feminine traits showed that he also identified with his mother, though he disrespected and denied her because of her weaknesses. And Murray believed that: 'There is some evidence that in Hitler's mind "Germany" is a mystical conception which stands for the ideal mother – a substitute for his own imperfect mother.'

He spoke of Germany as a beloved woman and identified with her from an early age, but went on to reject his entire family, clan and class – with the exception of his half-sister Angela, Geli's mother.

VIENNESE DAYS

Murray then discussed Hitler's days in Vienna. He depended for an account of this period on the recollections of Reinhold Hanisch, whom he had met in 1909. Five years older than Hitler, Hanisch took him under his wing when they both lived at the Meldemannstrasse public dormitory for men and they went into business together. Hitler painted postcards, posters and watercolours which Hanisch sold and they split the money. The problem was that when Hitler got a little cash he refused to work. According to Hanisch:

'I was often driven to despair by bringing in orders that he simply would not carry out. At Easter 1910, we earned forty kronen on a big order and we divided it equally. The next morning, when I came downstairs and asked for Hitler, I was told he had already left with Neumann, a Jew. ... After that I couldn't find him for a week. He was sightseeing Vienna with Neumann and spent much of the time in the museum. When I asked him what the matter was and whether we were going to keep on working, he answered that he must recuperate now, that he must have some leisure, that he was not a coolie. When the week was over, he no longer had any money.'

They fell out when Hitler accused Hanisch of keeping the money he had got for a picture. He had Hanisch arrested and appeared as a witness against him. Hanisch then spent seven days in prison. After serving as a soldier in World War I, Hanisch dabbled in art and petty theft. As Hitler rose to notoriety, Hanisch forged his pictures. When Hitler became chancellor in 1933, Heiden sought him out for an account of Hitler's years in Vienna. Hanisch was also interviewed by numerous national and international newspapers, even daring to contradict what Hitler had said in *Mein Kampf*.

'I've never seen him do hard work, yet I heard that he had laboured as a construction worker,' said Hanisch. 'Contractors employ only strong and powerful people.'

In December 1936, after trying to find a publisher for his memoir of his time with Hitler, Hanisch was arrested for selling Hitler fakes. He died after two months in prison, allegedly murdered by Hitler's henchmen. His memoir was published posthumously in 1939 by the American magazine *New Republic*.

Murray picked out two incidents he thought key in Hitler's world of rejection and aggression. One was that his landlady had thrown him out and made him homeless. The other was begging a few pennies from a drunken man who had raised his cane and insulted him. Hitler was very bitter about this.

Regarding this period, Murray said:

'Hitler wore a beard during this period and in his long overcoat looked very much like a certain type of Oriental Jew not uncommon in Vienna. Hitler had a number of Jewish acquaintances and sold postcards that he painted to Jewish dealers. There was no evidence during these first years of any hostility to Jews. Only later, after he had listened excitedly to the speeches of the anti-Semitic mayor, Lueger, did he become an avowed, and somewhat later a fanatical, anti-Semite himself.'

Karl Lueger was mayor of Vienna from 1897 until his death in March 1910. He was famous for his anti-Semitic rhetoric, but Jews did not suffer under his administration and it was thought that he only adopted racism as a pose to get votes. Asked why many of his friends were Jews, Lueger replied famously: 'I decide who is a Jew.'

While still in the homeless hostel, Hitler already had notions of starting a political party. Accused of theft, he left for Munich in 1913 to avoid jail. It was also said that he was in police records as a sex pervert, though Hitler claimed to be shocked by the sexual practices he saw in Vienna, with its numerous prostitutes. Hanisch said that Hitler had a purity complex. He also recalled Hitler telling him of an encounter with a milkmaid when he was still at school. She made advances and he fled, knocking over her milk churn in his haste. He later described his ideal woman as 'a cute, cuddly, naïve little thing – tender, sweet and stupid'.

He had already expressed his hatred of Austria and his love of Germany, where he longed to become a citizen. Throughout his five years in Vienna he had found himself constantly excluded. He was rejected by the Academy of Fine Arts, based on his inadequate education. Only the sons of well-to-do parents were deemed worthy of higher education. The fashionable world, of which he could not be a part, expressed a patronizing 'sympathy for the people', he thought.

'To me Vienna, the city which, to so many, is the epitome of innocent pleasure, a festive playground for merrymakers, represents, I am sorry to say, merely the living memory of the saddest period of my life,' he said.

POLITICAL EDUCATION

However, while in Vienna, Hitler had spent time in libraries studying history and had attended the Austrian parliament and political meetings. Taking a pragmatic view, he became preoccupied with the question: why does one political movement fail and another succeed? Again Murray asked why Hitler, when living among the proletariat, found the ideology of communism so repellent? But Hitler saw himself as someone who, 'through his own energy, works his way up from his previous social position to a higher one', saying 'this relentless struggle kills all pity. One's

S. Exc. Dr. C. Lueger's letzter Besuch im Hotel Panhans 24. Februar 1909 · Semmering.

Karl Lueger (next to nun) in an open-top carriage in the Alpine resort of Semmering, probably on his way to the railway station, 1909.

own painful scramble for existence suffocates the feeling of sympathy for the misery of those left behind.'

Murray observed: 'Brought up by such a father, it was natural for Adolf Hitler to envy and admire his social superiors and look with contempt upon those of a lower station.' The American editors of *Mein Kampf* added: 'Hitler, conscious of belonging to a higher social caste than his fellow-workers ... instinctively retreats from the idea of accepting solidarity with them.'

Hitler identified with the German nationalist movement and saw the internationalism of communism as an enemy. He was also an enthusiastic militarist and, as a social class, the military are antipathetic to communists generally. And he had reverence for the strong and contempt for the weak, so he favoured a stratified social system with the dictatorship of the elite. There was no compassion in his make-up, no sympathy for the underdog. His ideology was founded on the rise to power of nature's supermen and involved the relationship of dominance and submission among men.

FIRST WORLD WAR

When he joined the army, Hitler became the accepted member of a respected institution for the first time. It gave him grounds for pride and a sense of security. At last, he was at one with the German nation.

'There is no evidence that Hitler was ever in a front line trench,' said Murray.

However, he was a messenger, carrying important communiqués across ground shelled by the enemy and there can be no doubt that he showed courage in this role. He was one of four despatch runners among the sixty men from his regiment to be awarded the Iron Cross Second Class. The story was circulated that Hitler then won the Iron Cross First Class for single-handedly capturing fifteen French soldiers. Murray noted that there was no record of this incident in the War Department and said that the award was given after he had left the front, supposedly gassed in one of the last offensives of the Allies. It seems that Hitler was promised the award for carrying a message through heavy fire and was only given the medal after dogged petitioning.

Murray wrote that:

'Informants have commented on Hitler's marked subservience to the superior officers, offering to do their washing and performing other menial tasks, courting their good graces to such an extent that his comrades were disgusted. Hitler was the only man in his company never to receive any mail or packages from home, and at Christmas and occasions when others were receiving gifts and messages, he sulked moodily by himself.'

Again, he seemed to be courting rejection. It was also noted that, in four years of service, he was not promoted above the rank of corporal.

'The comment by one of his officers that he was a neurotic fellow is the only explanation that has been advanced,' said Murray.

Hitler was gassed in October 1918, but Murray did not think this was serious, rather

'a war neurosis, hysterical blindness, which also deprived him of his voice and perhaps his hearing. This psychosomatic illness was concomitant with the final defeat of his Mother Germany, and it was after hearing the news of her capitulation [that] he had his vision of his task as saviour. Suddenly his sight was restored.'

Hitler was also disturbed, and impressed, by the Allies' propaganda. 'Two years later, I was master in this craft,' he wrote.

CHANGED MAN

Murray remarked that many of the facts of Hitler's life after 1919 were common knowledge. However, he found a few points worthy of highlighting and quoted an informant saying that after Hitler was released from military hospital he was 'a stray dog looking for a master'. Again Murray thought he was embittered by rejection.

While still in the army, Hitler was assigned to indoctrinating soldiers. Suddenly he experienced success.

'Hitler's realization that he had the power to sway large masses of people was the second crucial fact, next to his revelation in the hospital while

Seated at far left with a cross above his head, Hitler is seen with fellow soldiers and obligatory dog during World War I, a time most of his key ideas came from.

blind, in determining his career,' said Murray, surmising that he had been making speeches in fantasy since boyhood. He had certainly done a good deal of informal haranguing 'first as adolescent leader of the young Nationalists at school, second as a ham politician among the derelicts of the Vienna slums, and third as a corporal behind the lines'.

His oratory now was of a different order and the defeat of Germany had made him determined to become a revolutionary. Key to his progress was Ernst Röhm, a superior officer with an upper-class background. Hitler envied his physical strength and social assurance and Murray thought that having the backing of such a figure gave Hitler a sense of security.

Up until the abortive Beer Hall Putsch of 1923, Hitler continued his conspicuous worship of and flattering subservience to officers, 'but from 1924 on, although he never entirely lost a certain embarrassment in the presence of his former superiors, there was a change from abasement to dominance and even arrogance in dealing with aristocrats and war lords,' wrote Murray.

'During the years from 1923 to 1933, Hitler's emotional outbursts, his tantrums of rage and indignation, his spells of weeping and threats of self-annihilation increased in frequency and intensity. This can be partly accounted for by the fact that they were effective in bringing his associates around to his point of view. Instead of antagonizing the group of revolutionists who with him were plotting to usurp power, these frightful orgies of passion served to intimidate them. Everyone sought to avoid topics that would bring about the fits.'

Among the reasons given for the cold-blooded purge of 1934, where hundreds of Nazis were murdered, were that the victims were 'disgusting homosexuals' and that they were plotting to seize power from him.

Murray noted that during the twenty years since 1923, rumours had periodically arisen to the effect that Hitler was enamoured of this or that young woman. These snippets were either fabricated or premature, since these liaisons were generally rather short-lived.

Night of the Long Knives – Hitler brought to heel Ernst Röhm's paramilitary organization, the SA, with its two million members.

'The one affair that stands out is that with a nineteen-year-old, Angela (Geli) Raubal, his niece. Hitler was often in her company and was pathologically jealous of any attentions shown her by other men. Two informants have stated positively that Hitler murdered the girl, but the official report was suicide. Whichever story is correct, however, we gain the impression of a peculiar and stormy relationship. Rumours have it that Hitler's sexual life, such as it is, demands a unique performance on the part of the women, the exact nature of which is a state secret.'

Murray tied this to Hitler's vaunted asceticism, noting that while he was a vegetarian, his food was served to him by the best chefs in Germany and that it was said he did not permanently give up meat until after the death of Geli.

PERSONALITY STRUCTURE

The report continued with an assessment of Hitler's personality structure.

'Hitler's ego is surprisingly weak,' said Murray, who said he lacked the ability to organize and co-ordinate his efforts. As a boy, he was aimless and unable to apply himself. During his time in Vienna, he had difficulty getting up in the morning and suffered from 'paralysis of the will'. While prescribing disciplined work for those around him, he lived like an artist or bohemian.

According to Rauschning, 'Hitler seems a man of tremendous willpower, but the appearance is deceptive. He is languid and apathetic by nature, and needs the stimulus of nervous excitement to rouse him out of chronic lethargy to spasmodic activity ...'

He was indecisive and was incapacitated by mental confusion until his inner voice spoke to him when the situation became threatening. Röhm said: 'Usually he solves suddenly, at the very last moment ... only because he vacillates and procrastinates.'

He was unable to control his emotions, though it was noted that he could turn his tantrums on and off at will. Nevertheless, 'such unmanly display of infantile intolerance to frustration, or tears and shrieks, is entirely out of keeping with his own ideal of the Iron Supermensch,' Murray said.

Hitler lacked objectivity, allowing his own projection to distort reality to the point of delusion. His writings and reported speeches exhibited a disorganization of ideas and verbal expression which at times verged on the pathological. He also lacked insight, having no capacity to admit his errors and defects, though this was politically expedient. Perhaps most difficult for those around him, he had an unbelievable capacity to lie and a disarming ability to claim total innocence of promises and assertions made only a moment before.

Murray contrasts these signs of weakness with the fact that Hitler had the power to do what he wanted to do, the power to resist the coercions of society and the power to resist the dictatorship of the conventional superego or conscience. He had initiative and self-sufficiency, the ability to take responsibility and direct others, the capacity to take account of the distant future when making decisions.

Summing this up, Murray said:

'Hitler operates on thalamic energy rather than on conscious will and rational planning. Possessed by fanatical passion he can accomplish things which those who act on cooler and more moderate plans fail to achieve. The force, in other words, comes from the id, and the ego is used in its service. This combination is typical of the gangster; Hitler is different from the ordinary type, having some of the attributes of the romantic artist. He is a compound, say, of Lord Byron and Al Capone.'

Explaining his terms, Murray said: 'Under the term id I am including all unconscious and psychic processes – principally affective and conative processes which emerge suddenly without voluntary effort and take possession of the ego but also unconscious intellective processes resulting in sudden judgments and decisions.'

Hitler would not have disagreed. He was clear on this point.

'We must distrust the intelligence and the conscience and must place our trust in our instincts,' he said. He talked of 'over-educated people, stuffed with knowledge and intellect, but bare of any sound instincts'. And in *Mein Kampf* he wrote: 'Of secondary importance is the training of mental abilities.'

Logic was abandoned and instinct was its own justification. In other words, Murray said, Hitler functioned like a creative artist, which was unusual in someone who had gone into politics. However, his dependence on these involuntary processes make him unable to make decisions about the hundred and one little matters that came up in his daily routine.

'Unless I have the inner incorruptible conviction: this is the solution, I do nothing. Not even if the whole Party tried to drive me to action, I will not act. I will wait, no matter what happens. But if the voice speaks then I know the time has come to act,' he said.

CASTLES IN THE AIR

Hanisch said that Hitler 'spent his time building castles in the air', while Rauschning had the impression that Hitler was not listening when he spoke and his thoughts were far away.

Murray quoted another informant, named only as Roberts, who believed that Hitler, wrapped up in his own dream world, was unaware of a large part of the practical activities and even the brutalities of his own party. He depended on the support of Goebbels, Göring and Himmler.

'Because of the tremendous downward pull of unconscious processes Hitler must often pull himself up by the bootstraps, as it were, to meet an emergency,' said Murray.

Hitler himself said: 'I follow my course with the precision and security of a sleepwalker.'

Murray also described the 'dynamic pattern of energy bolted up in him'.

'It is a rigid, fanatical, and incurable reservoir of the thalamic energies which, on release, have two or three times the potency that a normal man brings to bear upon any one reasonable object.'

His ego can call into play or check this unconscious complex.

'Hitler makes good use of his capacity to be possessed by the complex,' said Murray. 'He dramatizes it, whips it up, and intoxicated by the words that pour out of his mouth, deliriously gives vent to his passion.'

Murray said that Hitler felt that he was the object of divine protection, like many religious leaders. He compared Hitler to Joseph Smith, the founder of Mormonism, 'the chief difference being that Smith's voices gave him permission to free the sex instinct, whereas Hitler's voices encourage brutality and destruction'. He also compared Hitler to Mary Baker Eddy, the founder of Christian Science, who also heard voices.

Diagnosing a 'hysteroid personality', Murray said:

> 'Besides the definitely recorded hysterical attack of blindness and aphonia (in 1918), there are his paroxysms of emotion, his hallucinations, coming out of nightmares, his sudden revelations and hearing of inner voices, and the periods of day-dreaming and abstraction, all of which are reminiscent of hysterics, inspired and uninspired, of which the history of religion furnishes so many striking examples. Here he might be likened, perhaps, to Joan of Arc.'

PARANOID SCHIZOPHRENIA

Hitler also 'possessed a complete semi-delusional system characteristic of paranoid schizophrenia. ... The enormous banked-up hate and revengefulness in the man and the acts of cruelty which he is able to execute apparently without the normal recriminations of conscience are also symptomatic of schizophrenia.'

However, while it could be said that Hitler was an hysteric on the verge of schizophrenia, his success in imposing his delusional system on the German people was so phenomenal that he had remained within the boundaries of technical sanity.

When it came to his superego or conscience, Murray said that it seemed clear that Hitler was not an amoral brute like Göring or many of his followers, but his superego was repressed, 'the mechanisms of the ego being set up against its interference'. This was done by allying the ego to the instinctual forces of the id, but it took a great deal of physic energy to repress the superego and any feelings of guilt it might give rise to. This

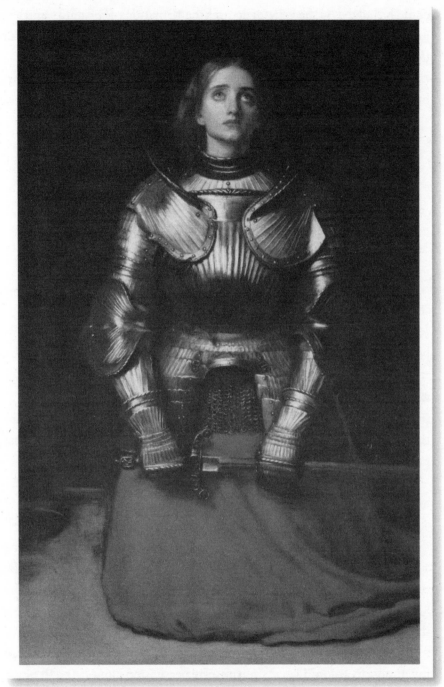

Joan of Arc, who heard voices and in this sense might be compared to
Adolf Hitler as a hysteroid personality.

could be judged by the vehemence of his affirmations of brutality and the justifications he felt called on to give for actions that appalled the rest of the world.

Hitler was not unconscious of what he was doing. Indeed, it was his purpose.

'I am freeing men from restraints of an intelligence that has taken charge; from the dirty degraded modifications of a chimera called conscience and morality and from the demands of a freedom and personal independence which only a very few can bear. We must be ruthless. We must regain our clear conscience as to ruthlessness. Only thus shall we purge our people of their softness and sentimental Philistinism and their degenerate delight in beer-swilling.'

He also said: 'I recognize no moral law in politics' and 'Conscience is a Jewish invention.'

Murray said that Hitler was posing as a Nietzschean anti-Christ who was going to create a new superego for mankind, the exact opposite of the one that had prevailed since the establishment of Christianity. But that pose was only for his close followers. To the world, he knew he must present a different face.

'Moral commonplaces are indispensable for the masses,' he said. 'Nothing is more mistaken than for a politician to pose as a non-moral superman.'

According to Murray at least, Hitler had not entirely conquered the superego that he acquired on the knee of his pious mother, at the Catholic monastery at Lambach and from his teachers at school. He said that the SA 'did not want to establish violence as its aim, but wanted to protect the messengers of the spiritual aim against oppression by violence'.

'I did not wish to carry out my purposes by force,' he said, 'instead I did my utmost to accomplish my purpose by persuasion alone.' And 'It never has been my intention to wage wars, but rather to build ...'

Speaking of the invasion of Poland, he said: 'I forbade the sacrifice of more human lives than was absolutely necessary.'

With the benefit of hindsight, we can see that these examples quoted by Murray cannot be taken at face value. At the Nuremberg Trials testimony was presented that showed Hitler planned for an aggressive war from the outset and several of the defendants were convicted because they had done nothing to stop him.

NIGHTMARES AND DEPRESSION

Murray conceded that Hitler did succeed in repressing his superego most of the time. He consciously and openly committed most of the crimes on the calendar, 'so much so that the diagnosis of "psychopathic personality" or "moral imbecile" seems almost justified'. But Murray insisted that a superego of sorts continued to operate unconsciously, citing his inability to sleep quietly for weeks after the Night of the Long Knives. Following the bloody purge, he prowled up and down restlessly at night, had nightmares and suffered depressions and thoughts of suicide.

According to Murray's hypothesis, many of Hitler's later acts of aggression could be attributed to his superego.

'Having once started on a career of brutality, he can only quiet the pain of a bad conscience by going on with ever greater ruthlessness to achieve successes, and so to demonstrate to himself and others that God approves of him and his methods,' Murray explained. This only worked if the outcome of these aggressions was successful. 'Failure will undoubtedly be followed by guilt feelings.'

For Murray, further evidence of superego activity came from Hitler's use of projection. While Hitler was frequently listless, he said: 'All passivity, all inertia … is senseless, inimical to life.' And while Hitler – indeed, all Nazi ideology – insisted that he was always right, he called intellectuals: 'These impudent rascals who always know everything better than anybody else.'

PARANOID DELUSION

Hitler claimed that he was governed by instinct and intuition, rather than reason, yet he condemned the people who were 'so feminine in their nature and attitude that their activities and thoughts are motivated less by sober consideration than by feeling and sentiment'.

While Hitler lied without a second thought, he condemned the Jews as 'the great masters of lying'. Although he hypnotized others with his stare, he complained of those that 'tried to pierce me even with their eyes'.

One of Hitler's favourite entertainments was private performances of nude dancing, but he condemned Soviet foreign minister Georgy Chicherin – and his staff of over two hundred Soviet Jews – for visiting the cabarets and watching 'naked dancers perform for his pleasure …'

Murray compiled a list of Hitler's descriptions of others that applied more accurately to himself. These included saying that the Social Democrats' doctrine consisted of egoism and hatred which 'could bring about the end of mankind' and that they directed 'a bombardment of lies and calumnies towards the adversary who seemed most dangerous'. Then he said that the Jews' entire activity was 'unrestricted by moral obligation'. 'We will not let the Jews slit our gullets and not defend ourselves,' he said. They 'dream of world domination'. He had talked himself hoarse about 'the destructiveness of the Marxist doctrine of irrationality'. And he calmly declared that the Allies were warmongers – 'for this peace proposal of mine,' he said, 'Mr Chamberlain … spat upon me before the eyes of the world.' Of the Poles, he said – 'the outstanding features of the Polish character were cruelty and lack of moral restraint'.

The list concluded with Murray's comment: 'The intensity and frequency of these projections amply justify the diagnosis of paranoid delusion.'

LIVED OUT HIS FANTASY

Murray also noted that 'Hitler is one of the relatively few men who has largely lived out his fantasy.'

Since being a schoolboy, he had admired Germany, particularly Prussia whose military prowess had helped bring about the unification of Germany in 1870. This would be completed at the *Anschluss* and the reincorporation of German-speaking people who had fallen outside the borders of the Reich after World War I.

He admired power, particularly that of the British with their vast empire, and by the time Murray's report was written had created an empire that rivalled it. And he admired great men such as Wagner and

Death comes for Adolf Hitler in this cartoon by D.R. Fitzpatrick from the
Denver Post **in 1943 (after Stalingrad).**

Mussolini and considered himself one of them. He took his portrait of Frederick the Great into the bunker with him.

Earlier in life he had shown deference towards his superiors. Now others showed him that deference. He admired only strength. For Hitler, strength was the only virtue. All human feelings were seen to be weakness and he believed that he had succeeded in banishing them. Hitler flattered himself that he had become 'the super superman, leading a nation of supermen who govern the globe'. This appealed to the German people, Murray said, because of the autocratic position of the father in the structure of the German family, systematic indoctrination in the home and schools and the position of Germany in Europe, encircled and for a long time eclipsed first by France and then by Great Britain.

Hitler's belief in terrorism was proved correct – up until that point at least.

'Brutality is respected,' he said. 'Brutality and physical strength. The plain man in the street respects nothing but brutal strength and ruthlessness.'

Murray noted that this was another example of self-projection 'and sums up in a nutshell the crux of Hitler's personality'. He went on to say:

'One will not be able to understand Hitler's personality, its extra-ordinary force, its maintenance this side [of] insanity, and its influence on the German people without taking full account of his emotional identification with an ideal Germany as he conceives it and the dedication of his efforts to the creation of such a Germany.'

Hitler was clear about how this social ideal would be brought about from the beginning. In *Mein Kampf* he wrote: 'The Nazi Party must not be the masses' slave, but their master.'

PLAYING THE ROLE

Murray believed that if Germany had already been in the grip of an iron man Hitler would have been willing to take his place in the system as a subordinate. But when he became dissatisfied with other political leaders, by degrees, he forced himself into the role that he believed someone had to fill.

Frederick the Great was one of Hitler's heroes. He turned Prussia into a great power and helped bring about the unification of Germany.

'It was as if a masochist, finding no one to play a role sufficiently sadistic to gratify his eroticism, were to decide to adopt that role himself. We find here the possibility of vicarious pleasure in either role. Listening to Hitler's words, we often get a certain sense of his identification with the sadist when he is adopting the submissive role, and his identification with the masochist when he is acting as a brutal tyrant.'

This change came about when he discovered his power as a speaker.

'The ambitious sadist, his infantile belief in omnipotence being reactivated by the hysterical approval of the masses, came into his own. We are dealing here with a personality who enviously admires his enemies. His enemies are those who dominate and oppose and frustrate him with force. He hates the person who embodies this force but he worships the force and as so patterns himself on the object of his hate.'

This explained why he was attracted to the Marxists and their methods for gaining power. He also admired the organizational skill of the Catholic Church and the British domination of India and their use of propaganda, along with American advertising techniques.

The closer he got to power, the more Hitler believed that he was the iron man who could save Germany, but earlier he had his doubts. At first, he resisted when Party members began addressing him as 'Mein Führer' – 'My Leader'. In 1922, he described himself as the 'drummer or rallier' of the cause and told one Party member: 'We are all St Johns. I wait for Christ.' He also told a group of industrialists: 'When the national front is so strong that it can reach for power, the Führer will be here too.'

Rauschning said Hitler told him: 'The new man is among us! He is here! Now are you satisfied? I will tell you a secret. I have seen the vision of the new man – fearless and formidable. I shrank from him.'

Murray said: 'Here is a suggestion that beyond the exercise of power there is a greater enjoyment – shrinking before a still greater force.'

BANISHING SELF-DOUBT

When Hitler came to power, self-doubt soon left him. Murray quotes Hitler saying: 'Who won the campaign in Poland? I did! Who gave the orders? I did! Who ordered the attack? *Ich, Ich, Ich, Ich*!'

He told Kurt Schuschnigg, the Austrian chancellor forced to resign before the *Anschluss*: 'Do you not realize that you are in the presence of the greatest German ever known to history?'

In *My New Order* Hitler said: 'I am one of the hardest men Germany has had for decades, perhaps for centuries, equipped with the greatest authority of any German leader ... but above all, I believe in my success. I believe in it unconditionally.'

Even before the Polish campaign, as he addressed his commanders, he said:

'In the last analysis there are only three great statesmen in the world, Stalin, I, and Mussolini ... our strength consists in our speed and in our brutality. Genghis Khan led millions of women and children to slaughter with premeditation and a happy heart. History sees in him solely the founder of a state. It's a matter of indifference to me what a weak western European civilization will say about me. I have issued the command – and I'll have anybody who utters but one word of criticism executed by a firing squad – that our war aim does not consist in reaching certain lines, but in the physical destruction of the enemy. Accordingly, I have placed my death-head formations in readiness ... with orders to them to send to death mercilessly and without compassion, men, women, and children of Polish derivation and language.'

By then Hitler saw himself as Germany's greatest strategist and warlord.

HITLER AS CHRIST

Hitler came to believe that he was the chosen instrument of God, the saviour of the German folk and the founder of a new spiritual era that was to endure, as Christ's kingdom was designed to endure, for a thousand years.

'It is not to be wondered at, therefore, that Hitler has often identified himself with Christ,' wrote Murray.

In *My New Order* he referred to himself as a Christian seizing 'the scourge to drive out of the Temple the brood of vipers and adders'.

'I believe I would be no Christian, but the very devil ... if I did not, as did our Lord two thousand years ago, turn against those by whom today this poor people is plundered and exploited.'

Murray noted that Hitler showed 'uncanny wisdom' in retaining the appearance of a typical lower-middle-class German. He wore the uniform of a common storm trooper or the ill-fitting suit of an average citizen, rather than yielding up to temptation to dress up in a fine uniform like Göring or in imperial robes like Napoleon. He maintained the image of a humble, ascetic man, even though it was known that he had a large portrait of himself as Führer above his desk in the Berghof.

THE SADIST

Hitler took a sadistic pleasure in the painful humiliation of his adversaries.

'There will be no peace in Europe until a body is hanging from every lamppost,' he said. Even if they did not win, he told Rauschning, 'we should drag half the world to destruction with us, and leave no one to triumph over Germany. There will not be another 1918.'

During the Night of the Long Knives, one of the first prisoners to be brought before Hitler was Röhm's aide-de-camp Count Spreti. According to Heiden: 'He made a gesture that Hitler interpreted as an attempt to reach for a gun. The Führer then hit him on the head with the iron end of a heavy whip, and kept hitting the young man's face and skull until he collapsed.'

ONE WITH GERMANY

Though Hitler often appeared to be a lone wolf – indeed adopting the name Wolf – he needed the masses around him. From the time he was a nationalist at school, he longed to be one of the idealized German people. Even at the flophouse in Vienna he talked of starting a party. Within the Nazi Party, he created an elite bodyguard, but he still reached out and identified with the idealized German folk. No one doubted his love for Germany, or his dedication to its cause.

Polish citizens are executed from right to left as a reprisal for the killing of a single German soldier, 1941.

Murray wrote:

> 'It was this feeling of oneness with Germany and the fact that he could identify his revengefulness with the need for aggression latent in the German nation which enabled him to hold his ground and this side [of] insanity. Once the Party had conquered the German people, he could function corporocentrically rather than egocentrically. It was this that saved him and won him adherents.'

It also allowed him to believe that, rather than imposing on the German people his vision of an idealized state, he was the mouthpiece for their deepest yearnings and, consequently, was doing their bidding.

Murray said that the evidence demonstrated that Hitler's energies would never have been fully brought to bear had it not been for Germany's defeat in World War I and its collapse afterwards. Up until that time, he had political convictions, but sufficient stimulus was lacking. Murray summed up Hitler's 'orientating thema', saying:

> 'The treacherous, overpowering, and contaminating, the weakening and depreciation, of a pure and noble object is the tragic spectacle which arouses the hero and incites him to agitate revenge. As Leader and Messiah, he compels the object, by sheer will and eloquence, to adopt a course of ruthless aggression, the goal being to annihilate the contaminator and aggressor, and so, guided by its almighty ruler and redeemer, to become supremely pure, powerful, and superior, and thus everlastingly respected. His work done, the hero relinquishes power and dies, revered as the progenitor of an uncorrupted and masterful race that will live on in fulfilment of his word.'

VOYEURISM

In Hitler's love of architecture, Murray spots a suggestion of voyeurism. In *Mein Kampf*, Hitler wrote:

> 'I had eyes for nothing but the buildings … all day long, from early morn until late at night, I ran from one sight to the next, for

what attracted me most of all were the buildings. For hours on end I would stand in front of the opera or admire the parliament buildings; the entire Ringstrasse affected me like a fairy tale out of the *Arabian Nights*.'

Murray said these buildings were the psychic equivalents of the mother he had lost, though Hitler was describing a visit to Vienna that took place before his mother's death. Murray was also reminded of the 'unique claustrum which Hitler had constructed for himself on the top of the mountain behind his retreat at Berchtesgaden'.

The Austrian parliament building in Vienna which sent Hitler into reverie and must have greatly contrasted with his lowly lodgings in the city.

COUNTERACTIVE NARCISSISM

'Counteractive narcissism' was the term Murray coined from the type of personality structure Hitler exhibited and he listed the common characteristics, giving examples:

1. **Narcisensitivity** – low tolerance of belittlement, depreciation, criticism, contradiction, mockery, failure; inability to take a joke; tendency to harbour grudges, not forgetting and forgiving. Hanisch

said Hitler could not stand criticism of his paintings and could not stand to be contradicted. He would get furious. He couldn't restrain himself, would scream and fidget with his hands. Rauschning recollected that Hitler was always looking around suspiciously, giving the impression that he wanted to see if anyone was laughing.

2. **Recognition (self-exhibition)** – self-display; extravagant demands for attention and applause; vainglory. 'Hitler's appearances at meetings and rallies are dramatized to the fullest extent. He is careful to have electric lights shining on him in such a way as to produce the most striking effects possible, etc., etc. However, one gets the impression the exhibitionism is limited to talking before a crowd – at which times it is extreme – but that ordinarily he is self-conscious and ill at ease, and does not particularly enjoy showing himself in public, although he must do this to maintain his power.'

3. **Autonomy (freedom)** – self-will; to insist on a sufficient area of liberty, on free thought, speech and action. Resistance or defiance in the face of forceful coercions or restraints; to combat tyranny. 'After his father's death he was given his own way and after leaving school became increasingly resistant to rules and regulations. He was never able to hold a job. He wanted to be an artist and live like a bohemian.'

4. **Dominance (self-sufficiency)** – when one is in a position of authority, to plan and make decisions without consulting others; to refuse to change an announced decision; to resent disagreements and interferences; to be annoyed by opposition; to insist on being sole ruler of one's province – home, business, political party, nation. Heiden, quoting Hitler: 'I am not contending for the favour of the masses … I alone lead the movement, and no one can impose conditions on me so long as I personally bear the responsibility for everything that occurs in the movement.'

5. **Refusal of subordinate position** – to avoid, refuse, or leave a position which does not do justice to one's felt powers or accomplishments;

to want to first place nothing (fusion with Autonomy). 'Hitler's refusal to accept membership of the cabinet in 1932. He insisted on complete power.'

6. **Reluctance to admit indebtedness** – to be disinclined to express gratitude or acknowledge help received, to deny or minimize the contribution of others. Rauschning: 'Hitler has always been a poseur. He remembers things he has heard and has a faculty of repeating them in such a way that the listener is led to believe that they are his own.'

7. **Counteractive achievements** – persistent efforts in the face of unexpected obstacles; or re-striving after a defeat; or repeated and enduring attempts to overcome fears, anxieties, deficiencies or defects; effort to defeat a once successful rival. Heiden: 'When others after a defeat would have gone home despondently, consoling themselves with the philosophic reflection that it was no use contending against adverse circumstances, Hitler delivered a second and a third assault with sullen defiance. When others after a success would have become more cautious because they would not dare put fortune to the proof too often and perhaps exhaust it, Hitler persisted and staked a bigger claim on destiny with every throw.' *Mein Kampf*: 'Only in the eternally regular use of force lies the preliminary condition to success.'

8. **Rejection (verbal depreciation)** – to belittle the worth of others, especially if they are superiors, rivals and potential critics (fusion of verbal Rejection and Aggression). Rauschning: 'Hitler distrusts everyone who tries to explain political economy to him. He believes that the intention is to dupe him, and he makes no secret of his contempt for this branch of science.' *Mein Kampf*: 'My mind was tormented by the question: Are these still human beings, worthy of being part of a great nation? … it brought me internal happiness to realize definitely that the Jew was no German. … armed in one's mind with confidence in the dear Lord and the unshakeable stupidity of the bourgeois.'

9. **Counteractive aggression** – to repay an insult in double measure – a tooth for a tooth; to revenge an injury; to attack opponents, superiors, and frustrators. (i) Verbal: to accuse, condemn, curse, damn, depreciate or mock an enemy to his face, or behind his back by criticism, slander, subtle undermining of prestige, smear campaign, etc. *Mein Kampf*: 'One can only succeed in winning the soul of a people if, apart from a positive fighting of one's own for one's own aims, one also destroys at the same time the supporter of the contrary.' (ii) Physical: to attack or kill the depreciating, injuring or frustrating object. Purge of 1934, anti-Semitism, wars, etc.

10. **Intradeference (compliance)** – obedience to own intuitions and impulses; self-trust; fidelity to own feelings, sentiments, tastes, judgments, experiences. *My New Order*: 'But I knew just the same that my place would be there where my inner voice directed me to go. … Nothing will move me to go another way but the way which experience, insight, and foresight tell me to go.'

11. **Creation and cathection of an ideal ego** – satisfaction with one's ideal, with the height of one's aspirations; identification with this ideal.

12. **Ideal ego intradeference (respect)** – self-esteem; satisfaction with conduct, abilities and accomplishments of self. *Mein Kampf*: 'I waited with pride and confidence to learn the result of my entrance examination. I was so convinced of my success that the announcement of my failure came like a bolt from the blue. … I was firmly convinced that some day I would make a name as an architect. … In those months, for the first time, I felt fully the whims of fortune which kept me at the front in a place where any lucky move on the part of a negro could shoot me down, while somewhere else I would have been able to render a different service to my country. For I was bold enough to believe even then that I would have succeeded in this.'

13. **Defendance** – to defend one's self-esteem verbally by offering excuses and justifications, by blaming others, by depreciating the judges, by

The persecution of Jews in the Warsaw Ghetto was one example of murder on an industrial scale superintended by the Nazis.

exalting other aspects of one's personality, etc. Hitler's prime method of defending the status of his self is by blaming others (extrapunitive reaction). Two other common methods are: (i) Connecting self with other (respectable or great) people, who have done the same, or had the same happen to them, or suffered from the same defect. *My New Order*: 'If we committed high treason, then countless others did the same. I deny all guilt so long as I do not find added to our little company those gentlemen who helped ...' (ii) Proclaiming worth of criticized part of self, or another part, or of self as a whole; to assert the merit of what others condemn; to balance a defect with an asset; to wipe out a failure by recalling one's successes in this or in some other field. *My New Order*: 'I believe that as a Nationalist Socialist I appear in the eyes of many bourgeois democrats as only a wild man. But as a wild man I still believe myself to be a better European. ... if a people is to become free it needs pride and will-power, defiance, hate, hate and once again hate.'

14. **Insult as stimulus** – it is characteristic of the proud counteractive type of personality that his energies are not engaged unless he has been insulted or injured or imagined himself belittled in some way. Thus the man of this sort will often actively seek such a stimulus. *Mein Kampf*: 'If we had been attacked at that time, nay, if one had only laughed at us, we would have been happy in both events. For the depressing thing was neither the one nor the other, but it was only the complete lack of attention we encountered at that time. This was true most of all for my person.'

15. **Compulsive criminality** – having started on a course of revengeful aggression instigated by a real or supposed insult the individual is often led to act or to plan actions which are opposed by his conscience. Therefore he is compelled, if he is to fulfil his resolution of revenge, to repress his superego. This often results in a condition of mounting unconscious guilt which must be further subdued by a repetition or extension of the criminal behaviour in order, as it were, to prove, by

the success attending this conduct, that it is favoured by fortune and hence right. This is demonstrated in Hitler's case and is an important dynamical principle of his personality. It is necessary for him to commit crimes, more crimes, in order to appease his superego. As soon as successful offensive action becomes impossible, the man will become a victim of a long-repressed superego, a condition which will lead to suicide or mental breakdown.

INFERIORITY COMPLEX

Murray said that almost all psychologists who had analysed Hitler's personality had interpreted it by referring to the formula of Austrian psychiatrist Alfred Adler, the progenitor of the inferiority complex, that 'craving for superiority comes out of unbearable feelings of inferiority'. Some of Hitler's non-psychological associates reached essentially the same conclusion.

Rauschning said: 'In the harshness and unexampled cynicism of Hitler there is something more than the repressed effect of hypersensitiveness which has handicapped its bearer. It is an urge to reprisal and vengeance, a truly Russian-nihilistic feeling.'

He also remarked on Hitler's unfathomable capacity to hate, saying: 'Every conversation, however unimportant, seemed to show that that man was filled with immeasurable hatred. Hatred of what? It was not easy to say. Almost anything might suddenly inflame his wrath and his hatred. He seemed always to feel the need of something to hate.'

Elsewhere Rauschning said: 'Hatred – personal hatred – rang out in his words, revenge for early years of poverty, for disappointed hopes, for a life of deprivation and humiliation.'

Heiden said: 'Anyone acquainted with the unhappy life of this lonely man knows why hatred and persecution mania guided his first political footsteps. In his heart he nursed a grudge against the world, and he vented it on guilty and innocent alike. His cracking voice, his jerky gait, his sawing gestures expressed a hatred of which all who saw him were conscious.'

CAUSES OF HITLER'S WOUNDED NARCISSISM

1. Physical inferiority – Hitler's youthful frailty and general bodily awkwardness and weakness
2. Aggressive dominance (insult) – abasement and humiliation of himself and his mother at the hands of his father, leading to desire for revenge
3. Rejection – by his father and by his mother when a young sibling arrived, leading to suprafiliation to Germany
4. Poverty and low social status – four years living among the derelicts of Vienna
5. Failure – to graduate from Realschule, to pass the entrance examination of the Academy of Fine Arts, to make a living in Vienna
6. Subordinate office, success of rivals – not being promoted beyond corporal when other younger men were being promoted aggravated his wounded pride
7. Sexual inferiority – Hitler's reported inability to have sexual intercourse, perhaps due to physical or psychic impotence
8. Breakdown of courage – Hitler's war neurosis was a sign of a breakdown of nervous stamina in the face of overwhelming odds, which was probably experienced by him as a humiliation in view of his ego ideal.

SELF-CONTEMPT

Hitler also exhibited self-contempt, extolling all the qualities that he lacked. He talked of the nobility of being a superior breed due to the process of natural selection. But he himself was from lowly stock, the son of an illegitimate peasant and a servant girl. Several members of the family were mentally retarded.

He had none of the attributes his experts ascribed to the Nordic race and could never have qualified to become one of his own elite guard.

'Strong and handsome must my young men be,' he said. 'I will have them fully trained in all physical exercises. I intend to have an athletic youth – that is the first and chief thing.'

Hitler himself never had the slightest aptitude for or interest in athletics.

He preached the sanctity of the family and the necessity of breeding more Germans, yet he was unmarried and had no children. He also preached 'my new order' and demanded punctilious discipline from his subordinates, though he was disorderly and self-willed.

According to Rauschning, he came close to admitting his inadequacies: 'We older ones are used up. Yes, we are old already. We are rotten to the marrow … we are cowardly and sentimental. We are bearing the burden of a humiliating past, and have in our blood the dull recognition of serfdom and servility.'

On another occasion, he said: 'All of us are suffering from the ailment of mixed, corrupted blood. How can we purify ourselves and make atonement?'

FEMININITY, PASSIVE HOMOSEXUALITY, MASOCHISM

1. Feminine component in Hitler's physical make-up
2. Feminine traits – sentimentality, emotionality, shrieking at the climax of his speeches, artistic inclinations, sudden collapses, occasional softness
3. Identification with his mother – Hitler believed he was going to die of cancer, suggesting an underlying empathic relationship
4. Abasement to superiors, particularly strong males
5. Cathexis of male symbols – Hitler liked conspicuous columns in architecture and paintings of stallions, never mares
6. Attraction to homosexuals, such as Röhm, followed by their murder
7. Homosexual panic, evidenced in reports of his nightmares. Rauschning: 'He shakes with fear, making the whole bed

vibrate. He shouts confused, totally unintelligible phrases. He gasps, as if imagining himself to be suffocating ... Hitler stood swaying in his room, looking wildly about him. "He! He! He's been here!" he gasped. His lips were blue. Sweat streamed down his face. Suddenly he began to reel off figures, and odd words and broken phrases, entirely devoid of any sense ... then he suddenly broke out "There, there! In the corner! Who's that?" He stamped and shrieked in the familiar way.'

A still of a naked discus thrower from Leni Riefenstahl's film, *Olympia*, 1936.

8. Need for abasement – Hitler quoted by Rauschning: 'I have seen the vision of the new man – fearless and formidable. I shrank from him.'

9. Intraggressive tendencies – pre-occupation with suicide and death

10. Cathexis for the Hitler Youth – Hitler quoted by Rauschning: 'Look at these young men and boys! What material! With them I can make a new world.' Hitler was also reported vaunting 'vanity in a beautiful body (to be encouraged by men wearing less clothes)'.

11. Overt homosexual relations – three male lovers mentioned by Rauschning, included Albert Förster, Gauleiter of Danzig
12. Repression of femininity – through identification with aggression and brutality

Albert Förster, Gauleiter of Danzig, 1941.

PERVERSE SEXUAL COMPLEXES

Murray said that by careful study of the three thousand metaphors found in *Mein Kampf* it was possible to work out the chief patterns of Hitler's emotional and perverse sexual complexes. His conclusions were verified by conversations with a man who had talked to two women Hitler had had relations with. While the discovery of these patterns was helpful to a psychiatrist trying to develop a complete formulation of Hitler's character and was, therefore, indirectly pertinent to the final diagnosis and predictions of his behaviour, it had no bearing on the political situation, so he left them out of his final report.

ORIGINS OF HITLER'S ANTI-SEMITISM

1. The influence of political thinkers and speakers like Karl Lueger, Nazi 'philosophers' Gottfried Feder and Dietrich Eckart and Wagner
2. Repressed hatred and need for a scapegoat to vent it on
3. Rejection of his own possible Jewish heritage
4. Suitable subject to project his own traits on to, such as his physical timidity, sensitivity and polymorphous sexual impulses
5. The need to create a common enemy until military forces were ready to go to war
6. Directing aggression towards a common enemy would diminish the likelihood of it being turned on him
7. His militarism – Jewish people were identified as being anti-militarist
8. The Fascist advocacy of the aggressive drive over the acquisitive drive that Jews were generally identified with
9. His substitution of power and glory for peace and prosperity – the materialist goals Jews and communists were associated with
10. The substitution of the Nazis' fanatical irrationality for the intellectual relativism well-educated Jews embodied
11. His political principle of focusing hostility on a single enemy at a time, thereby increasing its intensity

STRENGTHS

Instead, he went on to Hitler's strengths. These included a full appreciation of the importance of the masses in the success of any movement and recognizing the value of winning the support of youth.

He could identify, through feeling, the deepest needs and sentiments of the average German and could give passionate expression to those longings. He could also appeal to both the most primitive and the most ideal inclinations in his audience, arousing the basest instincts, yet cloaking them with nobility, justifying all actions as a means to attain an ideal goal. Men would only die for an ideal that was capable of surviving beyond their generation.

Hitler also appreciated that the masses were as hungry for a sustaining ideology as they were for daily bread. Using his ability to analyse complex social conditions into a few dominant forces, he was then able to portray conflicting human forces in vivid, concrete imagery that was understandable and moving to the ordinary man.

He had the ability to draw on the traditions of people and, by reference to great classical and mythological themes, evoke the deepest unconscious emotions in his audience. Political action did not take place unless the emotions were involved. To do that, he brought artistry and dramatic intensity to his meetings and rallies.

As the bearer of the people's burdens and the vanguard of their future, he evoked their sympathy, concern and protectiveness. Women particularly felt tender and compassionate towards him. His bodyguard too felt intensely protective. They felt that he was single-mindedly dedicated to his mission and his vision of the future. He adhered to a few principles and one common goal with a fanatical stubbornness and his self-confidence evoked a sense of infallibility.

Surrounding himself with devoted aides whose talents complemented his own, he had mastered the art of political organization. He approached politics and social change as an artist, depending solely on his subconscious.

'Most of the world will concede that Hitler was a tactical genius,' said Murray. He quoted conservative industrialist and Hitler's early financier Fritz Thyssen, who said: 'Sometimes his intelligence is astonishing … miraculous political intuition, devoid of all moral sense, but extraordinarily precise. Even in a very complex situation he discerns what is possible and what is not.'

What made it easy for him was that he had removed conscience from making political decisions. He boasted that he had learned to use terror from the communists, but employed it more effectively than his instructors. He was also master of the art of propaganda. His rules

Transformation of the local custom of 'begging for eggs' into the 'expulsion of the Jews' in the village of Leissling, Saxony, 1936.

were simple – never admit any fault or mistake; never accept blame; concentrate on one enemy at a time; blame that enemy for everything that goes wrong; and take advantage of every opportunity to raise a political whirlwind.

PREDICTIONS

Murray concluded with some predictions, assuming that the Allied nations would close in on Germany, there would be an increasing number of military setbacks in the field and a defeatist spirit would spread among the German people as one industrial centre after another was devastated.

First, he thought that Hitler would become increasingly neurotic, so his capacity to make the right decision, devise an effective strategy and encourage his people would diminish steadily. He thought he had already detected signs of a breakdown of psychic strength. Hitler appeared in public rarely and when he did his words were seldom inspiring. Several times there had been rumours that he had retired to Berchtesgaden, suffering from some nervous ailment.

Whether that was true or not, he would experience more hysterical seizures and be tormented by nightmares and depression. But after a period of recuperation in the mountains, he would return with a new plan for an aggressive offensive. If his military staff opposed it, he would assume command himself and lead his troops on another desperate assault against the Russian lines.

'If unsuccessful, he will have more nervous seizures, relinquish command, and again retreat to Berchtesgaden,' said Murray. 'Hitler has no capacity for sustained defence.'

He would speak less and less in public, as he could not face his people if his star was not ascending. He could only speak when he anticipated progress or after a victory. The Russians had shattered Hitler's confidence and without confidence he was paralyzed.

'If he stood before his followers now he would probably weep,' said Murray.

He would become increasingly fearful of being poisoned, shot or betrayed. As he became less of a leader, others would take over. This would lead to dissension between other top Nazis and between the Party

Grand finale of the Nuremberg Rally, 1935: national service had just been reintroduced along with the anti-Semitic Nuremberg laws.

and the military leadership. Nevertheless, the public would be kept in ignorance of his failing nerves for as long as possible, and they would not easily lose faith in him. While they could expect to hear nothing of him for a while, he was likely to reappear unheralded with some new plan.

Hitler might go insane. Already on the borderline, failure and frustration might push him over the edge. Even if the truth were kept from the people, Germany would lose its greatest source of strength. Morale would rapidly deteriorate as rumours spread. This would be the best outcome for the Allies as he would probably fall into their hands and the legend of the hero would be dead.

A worse outcome would be if he led his elite troops into battle against the Russians and got killed. This would inspire others to fight on fanatically. He would live on in the hearts of his countrymen as a valiant hero.

'He is very likely to choose this course,' said Murray.

Hitler had threatened to commit suicide on numerous occasions. Murray thought Hitler would find a dramatic way of doing this, possibly at the Berghof. He might poison himself and have it announced that he had died of cancer or some other incurable illness.

It was unlikely that he would seek refuge in a neutral country, unless tricked into it. He might be overthrown by the military or a revolutionary faction and be imprisoned, which Murray thought would be the most desirable outcome. Otherwise, in the course of the war, Hitler might fall into Allied hands, which would pose its own problems.

CHAPTER 5
Psychological Profiling

Professor Murray also contributed to a report by psychoanalyst Walter C. Langer, who led a team of psychologists and researchers. They spent five months interviewing key informants and compiled over a thousand pages of background research that became known as 'The Hitler Source Book'. His report led to the establishment of the CIA's profiling unit.

Langer had served in Europe during World War I and remembered how poor the Allies' psychological warfare efforts had been. In August 1941, as America's involvement in World War II was looming, he dashed off a letter to William J. 'Wild Bill' Donovan, who had recently been appointed head of the Office of Coordinator of Information, a new agency that compiled intelligence from existing sources.

Donovan invited him to Washington and asked him to lead a project to counter the anti-war movement, particularly among young men who might be expected to be drafted. His efforts were quickly overcome by the outrage that spread across the country following the attack on Pearl Harbor.

With America now at war – not just with Japan, but Germany and Italy as well – Donovan became head of the newly created Office of Strategic Services (OSS) and kept Langer on. Sometime in the spring of 1943, Donovan asked Langer what he made of Adolf Hitler. Langer had been studying in Germany and Austria in 1937 and 1938. During the *Anschluss*, he had witnessed Hitler's triumphant entry into Vienna, had heard him speak and had watched the audience's reaction. He had also observed the Nazi machine in action, persecuting the Jews, making mass arrests and creating a rigidly regimented society.

Donovan asked Langer to come up with a psychological profile of Hitler. He wanted to know what made him tick. Langer pointed out that this would be difficult. What was known about Hitler, though extensive, was unreliable and neither psychological nor psychoanalytic techniques were designed for such an undertaking, nor were they readily adaptable. Donovan was undeterred.

'Give it a try and see what you come up with,' he said. 'Hire what help you need and get it down as soon as possible. Keep it brief and make it readable to the layman.'

INTERVIEWING WITNESSES

While three psychoanalytically trained research workers combed the literature on file in the New York Public Library, Langer scoured the US and Canada for people who had had more than a passing contact with Hitler at some period of his life and interviewed them at length.

Interviewees included Hitler's nephew William Patrick Hitler, his family physician, Dr Eduard Bloch, who had treated his mother's cancer, Hitler's confidant in the Munich years Ernst Hanfstaengl, Hermann Rauschning, former German spy Princess Stephanie von Hohenlohe, Otto Strasser, Richard Wagner's granddaughter Friedelinde and early supporter Kurt Ludecke.

He kept the interviews as informal as possible. As many of the informants were held in detention camps due to their Nazi affiliations, they seized the opportunity to disavow any connection to Hitler. But once Langer had set them at ease, assuring them that he was not gathering information to justify their incarceration, they spoke more freely.

Langer encouraged interviewees to recall specific incidents, rather than dwell on generalities or personal conclusions. He wanted to know what Hitler said or did, what his attitude was, how he acted, whether there was anything unusual about his behaviour. This was time-consuming, but it produced a wealth of first-hand material not generally available through other sources at the time.

'When a halt was called on further research we had accumulated over eleven hundred single-spaced typewritten pages of excerpted quotations that appeared relevant,' said Langer. 'This mass of raw material was to serve as the base for our analysis of Hitler and his relationship with the German people. It became known as "The Hitler Source Book".'

COLLABORATION

Psychoanalysis unusually required the presence of the patient and their co-operation in relating whatever came to mind. This could hardly be the case for Langer's analysis of Adolf Hitler. To tackle that problem, Langer said:

'During the forty-five years since Freud had first discovered the psychoanalytic technique of exploration, a considerable number of persons suffering from wide and varied disorders had been psychoanalysed, and a wealth of clinical findings had been accumulated. From these findings, a theory of personality structure had been developed which sought to explain different character types in terms of early emotional development and subsequent cultural influences. This fund of knowledge, together with our own clinical findings, would have set the guidelines for our screening process.'

To do this he collaborated with three other experienced psychoanalysts. These were Professor Murray, Dr Ernst Kris of the New School for Social Research and Dr Bertram D. Lewin of the New York Psychoanalytic Institute. After a survey of the raw material, they made the preliminary diagnosis that Hitler was a neurotic psychopath. However, one of the collaborators found that they could not attend the evaluation meetings in New York.

'The only contribution he was able to make to the study was his agreement with our diagnosis and a verbal affirmation that Hitler's perversion, as reported, was highly probable in the light of his own clinical experience,' Langer said.

Langer also said that after he had finished his report he visited noted

Princess Stephanie von Hohenlohe was one of the people interviewed by Walter C. Langer regarding Adolf Hitler.

psychoanalyst Dr Jenny Waelder at her home in Bethesda, Maryland. During the course of their conversation, she asked him what he had been able to find out about Hitler's childhood.

'Without attempting to be orderly, I related the material as it came to mind, but omitted any appraisal of its possible significance. She listened intently for a while and then interrupted me, saying, "Now I know what his perversion is." At first I thought she was joking. She was, however, very serious and insisted she knew the perversion. To my utter amazement she was right! I asked on what basis she had reached this astonishing conclusion to which she replied, "It just came to me out of my clinical experiments."'

Langer complained that the powers that be had little comprehension of the magnitude of the project and were constantly urging him to finish it. He insisted that he was doing his best, but a deadline was set for the late summer of 1943 – then only a month away. As a result, any further collaboration was abandoned. Langer set about writing the report, finishing it just one hour before the Federal Express courier was due to leave for Washington on the night before the deadline. The whole thing had taken eight months.

In the preface to his report, Dr Langer wrote:

'This study is not propagandistic in any sense of the term. It represents an attempt to screen the wealth of contradictory, conflicting and unreliable material concerning Hitler into strata which will be helpful to the policy-makers and those who wish to frame counter-propaganda.'

INSIGHT

The first three parts were purely descriptive and dealt with the man as he appeared to himself, as he had been portrayed to the German people and as he was known to his associates. These segments contained the basic material for the psychological analyses in the sections that follow, when Langer attempted to understand Hitler as a person and fathom the motivations underlying his actions. The report concluded with a piece predicting Hitler's future behaviour.

'The material available for such an analysis is extremely scant and spotty. Fortunately, we have had at our disposal a number of informants who knew Hitler well and who have been willing to cooperate to the best of their abilities. The study would have been entirely impossible were it not for the fact that there is a relatively high degree of agreement in the descriptions of Hitler's behaviour, sentiments and attitudes given by these informants. With this as a basis it seemed worthwhile to proceed with the study filling in the lacunae with knowledge gained from clinical experience in dealing with individuals of the same type. This is not an entirely satisfactory procedure, from a scientific point of view, but it is the only feasible method at the present time. Throughout the study we have tried to be as objective as possible in evaluating his strengths as well as his weaknesses...

'It is hoped that the study may be helpful in gaining a deeper insight into Adolph Hitler and the German people and that it may serve as a guide for our propaganda activities as well as our future dealings with them.'

While Langer wished he had had more time to revise the draft and discuss his conclusions with his colleagues, the OSS seemed pleased with the results. A limited number of copies were printed, classified 'Secret' and distributed to the top brass. Langer never discovered who had read it. However, his brother, historian William L. Langer, was once introduced to Lord Halifax, the British ambassador to the US during the war, who said: 'Langer? Langer? You must be the author of the interesting study of Hitler that I read some time back.'

Walter Langer thought it was unlikely that Halifax had been on the original distribution list, but assumed that either the president or the secretary of state had thought it sufficiently important to hand it on to the British.

Soon after he submitted his report, Langer was asked to translate it into

German, but never discovered why. He did not think that it had any effect on the conduct of the war, but that was not its purpose. It came too late and, in any case, the outcome was decided on the battlefield.

'The goal we hoped to achieve was the presentation of an unbiased and professional psychological appraisal of Hitler,' he said, 'which might serve as a common basis for any decisions in the future.'

While admitting his naivety in diplomatic matters, Langer said:

'I like to believe that if such a study of Hitler had been made years earlier, under less tension, and with more opportunity to gather first-hand information, there might not have been a Munich; a similar study of Stalin might have produced a different Yalta; one of Castro might have prevented the Cuban situation; and one of President Diem might have prevented our deep involvement in Vietnam.'

After the war, Langer assumed that many of the copies were destroyed. Friends and colleagues urged him to publish it, but it remained classified so there was little he could do, other than to bequeath his own personal copy to Harvard University Library so that it would not be lost completely to future historians.

In 1969, he discovered that a copy had been turned over to the National Archives. It had been read by another academic and so was effectively declassified. Langer then went ahead and published his work in 1972 as *The Mind of Hitler: The Secret Wartime Report*, with a foreword by his brother William and an afterword by psychohistorian Robert G.L. Waite, Brown Professor of History at Williams College, who called the report 'fascinating … a significant and suggestive interpretation which no serious student of Hitler will ignore'.

As Langer collaborated with Murray, he covered much of the same ground, but with the additional material from the interviews he conducted he could come to much firmer conclusions.

THE SLEEPWALKER

In part one of his report – 'Hitler as He Believes Himself to Be' – Langer, like Murray, was struck that Hitler described himself as a 'sleepwalker', a remark made during the reoccupation of the Rhineland in March 1936, a decision he took against the advice of his generals.

'Even at that time it struck the world as an unusual statement for the undisputed leader of sixty-seven million people to make at the time of an international crisis,' said Langer. 'Hitler meant it to be a form of reassurance for his more wary followers who questioned the wisdom of his course.'

Already his sleepwalking had led him unerringly to a pinnacle of success and power never reached before. But by the time Langer was writing his report, things were turning against him and he stood on the brink of disaster. Langer said: 'He will go down in history as the most worshipped and the most despised man the world has ever known.'

Langer repeated Hitler's assertion that he was 'the greatest German of all time' and that he could not be mistaken – 'What I do and say is historical.'

He picked up other grandiose statements. According to Rauschning, Hitler said:

'I do not play at war. I do not allow the "generals" to give me orders. The war is conducted by me. The precise moment to attack will be determined by me. There will be only one time that will be truly auspicious, and I will wait for it with inflexible determination. And I will not pass it by.'

He also thought himself outstanding in jurisprudence, telling the Reichstag: 'For the last twenty-four hours I was the supreme court of the German people.'

His failure to follow a career in architecture did not stop him sketching plans for huge buildings and remodelling entire cities. And although he had failed to get into art school, he was the final arbiter in artistic matters. After the verdicts of a three-man committee he appointed failed to please him, he fired them and took over the job himself.

He was, of course, 'one of the hardest men in history' who believed in his own success 'unconditionally'.

In October 1938, the French ambassador to Berlin, André François-Poncet, said:

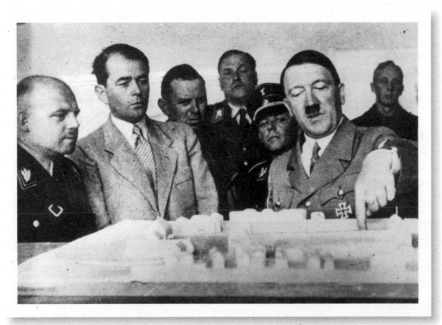

Hitler discussing his grand designs for a new administrative building in Weimar, 1936. His architect, Albert Speer, is at second left.

'His faith in his own genius, in his instinct, or as one might say, in his star, is boundless. Those who surround him are the first to admit that he now thinks himself infallible and invincible. That explains why he can no longer bear either criticism or contradiction. To contradict him is in his eyes a crime of *lèse-majesté*; opposition to his plans, from whatever side it may come, is a definite sacrilege, to which the only reply is an immediate and striking display of his omnipotence.'

The British ambassador, Sir Nevile Henderson, said: 'When I first met him, his logic and sense of realities had impressed me, but as time went on he appeared to me to become more and more unreasonable and more and more convinced of his own infallibility and greatness.'

DIVINE PROVIDENCE

Langer dismissed the idea that Hitler possessed this great confidence because he was a follower of astrology. In fact, he had outlawed it in Germany, perhaps fearing that horoscopes would unconsciously influence him. However, in the early 1920s Hitler took lessons in mass psychology, public speaking and the dramatic staging of meetings from a man named Hanussen, who was a practising astrologer and may have introduced him to his group. And if their predictions supported him, he used them.

Hitler was against reason and the intellect, saying: 'I carry out the commands that Providence has laid upon me.'

Later he said: 'No power on earth can shake the German Reich now, Divine Providence has willed it that I carry through the fulfilment of the Germanic task.'

He was commanded only by his inner voice – 'If the voice speaks, then I know the time has come to act.'

Langer noted that Hitler had felt he was in the hands of destiny for a long time. One of his comrades in 1915 said: 'Just before Christmas, he commented that we would one day hear a lot from him. We only had to wait until his time had come.'

Hitler reported several instances from the war that made him feel that he was under divine protection. In one, he said:

'I was eating my dinner in a trench with several comrades. Suddenly a voice seemed to be saying to me, "Get up and go over there." It was so clear and insistent that I obeyed automatically, as if it had been a military order. I rose at once to my feet and walked twenty yards along the trench carrying my dinner in its tin can with me. Then I sat down to go on eating, my mind being once more at rest. Hardly had I done so when a flash and deafening report came from the part of the trench I had just left. A stray shell had burst over the group in which I had been sitting, and every member of it was killed.'

Then when he was in hospital at the end of the war, he said: 'When I was confined to bed, the idea came to me that I would liberate Germany, that I would make it great. I knew immediately that it would be realized.'

THE DRUMMER

It was noted that in his early days in Munich, Hitler referred to himself modestly as 'a drummer'. However, in court after the Beer Hall Putsch failed, he said:

'You may as well accept the conviction that I do not regard a ministerial position as worth striving for. I do not consider it worthwhile for a great man to want his name in history only by becoming a minister. From the first day, I had a thousand times more in mind: I wanted to be the annihilator of Marxism. I shall solve the task, and when I solve it, then to me the ministerial title would be a trivial matter. The first time when I stood in front of Richard Wagner's tomb my heart was filled with pride. Here rests a man who ruled out an inscription such as: Here lies Privy Councillor Chief Conductor, His Excellency Baron Richard von Wagner. I was proud of this man, and so many men in German history were satisfied to leave their name to history, not their title.

Massed crowds bring a tram to a standstill in Marienplatz, Munich during the Putsch, 1923.

It was not modesty that made me want to be the "drummer". That is of the utmost importance, the rest is bagatelle.'

After his stay in Landsberg prison, where he dictated the first volume of *Mein Kampf*, Hitler no longer called himself the drummer, though he occasionally referred to himself as 'a voice crying in the wilderness' – that is, John the Baptist. But more often he would be called the Führer, the title chosen for him by Rudolf Hess, who had transcribed *Mein Kampf* and became deputy Party leader.

THE MESSIAH

Soon he thought of himself as the Messiah and references to the Bible and comparisons to Christ became frequent. According to Ernst Hanfstaengl, he said:

'When I came to Berlin a few weeks ago and looked at the traffic in the Kurfuerstendamm, the luxury, the perversion, the iniquity, the wanton display, and the Jewish materialism disgusted me so thoroughly, that I was almost beside myself. I nearly imagined myself to be Jesus Christ when He came to His Father's temple and found it taken by the money-changers. I can well imagine how He felt when He seized a whip and scourged them out.'

Early supporter Dietrich Eckart said: 'When a man gets to the point of identifying himself with Jesus Christ, then he is ripe for an insane asylum.'
The speech must have been before 26 December 1923, when Eckart died.
Brought up a Catholic, Hitler quit the Church after the war and he replaced the Christ he considered soft and weak with a harder model. In *My New Order*, he said:

'My feeling as a Christian points me to my Lord and Saviour as a fighter. It points me to the man who once in loneliness, surrounded by only a few followers, recognized these Jews for what they were and summoned me to fight against them and who, God's truth! was greatest not as a sufferer but as a fighter. In boundless love, as a Christian and as a man, I read through the passage which tells us how the Lord rose at last in His might and seized the scourge to drive out of the Temple the brood of vipers and adders. How terrific was the fight for the world against the Jewish poison.'

Langer also quoted Rauschning saying that Hitler referred with contempt to 'the Jewish Christ-creed with its effeminate pity-ethics'. Langer speculated whether Hitler intended to start a new religion. When addressed with the salutation 'Heil Hitler, our Saviour', he would bow slightly as if he believed it. He considered himself the 'Chosen One' and surrounded himself with his own portraits. Even before the war, it was clear that he wanted his name to ring down the ages. American journalist Karl von Wiegand wrote in April 1939: 'In vital matters, Hitler is far from unmindful of the name and record of success and failure he will leave to posterity.'

IMMORTALITY

Hitler believed that he must appear immortal to the German people. Everything must be a gigantic monument to him. The autobahns were known as 'Hitler Highways' and were to last longer than the road Napoleon built.

'He must always be doing the impossible and leaving his mark on the country,' said Langer. 'This is one of the ways in which he hopes to stay alive in the minds of the German people for generations to come.'

He planned a mausoleum 700 ft (213 m) high. After the invasion of France in 1940, Hitler went to Paris and visited Napoleon's tomb in the Dôme des Invalides, which is viewed from a gallery above. It was reported that Hitler said suddenly:

'I shall never make such a mistake. I know how to keep my hold on people after I have passed on. I shall be the Führer they look up at and go home to talk of and remember. My life shall not end in the mere form of death. It will, on the contrary, begin then.'

It was thought that his mountain-top Eagle's Nest had been built as a mausoleum, but abandoned for something even more grandiose.

The Eagle's Nest was originally built as a teahouse for Hitler's 50th birthday; its lofty position may have added to his delusions of grandeur.

Visiting Rome in 1938, he said that in a thousand years' time his monuments would not be in ruins. In 1933, he said that it would take twenty-two years before things were in good enough shape to hand over to a successor.

It was thought that he would then sit down and write the great bible of National Socialism that would endure forever. Early on Röhm said: 'Even today, the thing he would like best is to sit in the mountains and play God.'

Langer said of Hitler:

'A survey of all the evidence forces us to conclude that Hitler believes himself to be destined to become the Immortal Hitler, chosen by God to be the New Deliverer of Germany and the Founder of a new social order for the world. He firmly believes this and is certain ... he will finally attain that goal.'

American journalist Howard K. Smith, who had interviewed Hitler and was flung out of Germany on the day before Pearl Harbor, said: 'I was convinced that of all the millions on whom the Hitler Myth had fastened itself, the most carried away was Adolf Hitler himself.'

THE IMAGE

In part two of his report, Langer tried to describe 'Hitler as the German People Know Him'. Though thousands had seen him in person, their knowledge was limited by the tightly controlled press. Once more, Langer pointed out that physically Hitler was not a very imposing figure, far from the Platonic ideal of a great leader, and echoed others by saying he would not pass the requirements of his own elite guard. Smith called Hitler 'the apotheosis of the little man', funny-looking, self-conscious and unsure of himself. But posters and newsreels showed a fairly good-looking individual with a very determined attitude.

'These have undoubtedly, in the course of time, blotted out any unfavourable impression he may have created as a real person in the past,' said Langer. 'The physical Hitler most Germans know now is a fairly presentable individual.'

HIS VOICE

In the age of the radio, most people knew him through his voice and his speeches, where his power lay in telling an audience what they wanted to hear and manipulating their emotions.

Otto Strasser said:

'Hitler responds to the vibration of the human heart with the delicacy of a seismograph ... enabling him, with a certainty with which no conscious gift could endow him, to act as a loudspeaker proclaiming the most secret desires, the least permissible instincts, the suffering and personal revolts of a whole nation.'

As the subject of his speeches before he came to power never varied, people came to hear him speak over and over again because he was a showman. His speeches were scheduled for late in the evening when

After the German occupation of the Rhineland, Hitler holds forth to the municipal convention hall of Frankfurt am Main, 1936.

audiences would be tired and susceptible. They would be warmed up by a short talk before he arrived. Then Hitler would appear in the door at the back of the hall, before marching to the speaker's table.

'The beginning is slow and halting. Gradually he warms up when the spiritual atmosphere of the great crowd is engendered. For he responds to this metaphysical contact in such a way that each member of the multitude feels bound to him by an individual link of sympathy,' wrote pro-Fascist *Daily Mail* journalist George Ward Price, who had been introduced to Hitler by Lord Rothermere.

'Through all this, the listener seems to identify himself with Hitler's voice which becomes the voice of Germany,' said Langer.

He also noted that Hitler was a man of mystery. The secrecy he maintained around his personal life became a fertile ground on which to build a myth or legend. Meanwhile, the Nazi propaganda machine sought to portray him as something 'extra-human'. If he did not drink, smoke or eat meat, this was because such things were not worthy of the Führer. He needed to devote himself completely to the creation of the new German Reich. It also showed that he had enormous willpower and self-discipline.

The same went for sex. Von Wiegand wrote that Hitler 'has a profound contempt for the weakness in men for sex and the fools that it makes of them'. He would never marry and Germany was his only bride. But he was tolerant of that weakness in others. When a young Austrian girl wept because she could not get married after her fiancé had been sacked for his Nazi principles, he found the young man a job and furnished a flat for them, even buying them a baby's cot.

GREAT COMFORTER

The Nazi press also made great play of his love of children and animals. He was gentle, kind and helpful to all who needed him. He was the 'Great Comforter' to any German who had lost a relative and remained just 'one of the boys', as he had been when he founded the Party, happiest revisiting the old haunts in Munich or catching up with old friends.

When he came to power he continued wearing the same old trench coat and slouch hat, or the uniform of a simple storm trooper. He was still a worker with the interests of the working classes at heart, working tirelessly for them, taking no advantage of the luxuries his position afforded.

Langer quoted one young Nazi saying:

'I would die for Hitler, but I would not change places with Hitler. At least when I wake every morning I can say, "Heil Hitler!", but this man, he has no fun in life. No smoking, no drinking, no women! – only work, until he falls asleep at night.'

Even ordinary scruples did not get in his way. His propagandists made him out to be both infallible and incorruptible. He was a man of peace, who would not spill a drop of blood if it could be avoided and he showed great patience with the Western democracies, and with Czechoslovakia and Poland. A builder and an artist, he just wanted to be left alone to work out Germany's destiny. Not that he was a coward when it came to a fight. He had been awarded the Iron Cross First Class, though the story of how he had won it varied.

Langer included in his report a paragraph from Austrian journalist Erich Czech-Jochberg's 1933 book *Adolf Hitler and His Staff*:

'Next comes Hitler himself: Hitler is a man without compromise. Above all he knows no compromise with himself. He has one single thought that guides him: to resurrect Germany. This idea suppresses everything else. He knows no private life. He knows family life no more than he knows vice. He is the embodiment of the National will. The knighthood of a holy goal which can be climaxed by no man: Germany! … Hitler … surprises (with) his geniality. The tranquillity and strength radiate, almost physically, from this man. In his presence others grow. How he reads to everything! … His features harden and the words drop as stones … classical solemnity with which Hitler and his surrounding group of co-workers consider their mission has very few parallels in world history.'

Then there was a quotation from *The Hitler Nobody Knows* by his official photographer Heinrich Hoffmann:

Uncle Adolf clings on to Uschi Schneider, daughter of Herta Schneider, an old friend of Eva Braun, at the Berghof, 1942.

'Also in private matters of exemplary behaviour and human greatness ... whether Hitler ... is met with cheers by street-workers, or moved and shocked stands at the bed of his murdered companions, he is always surrounded by this grandeur and deepest humaneness ... this unique personality ... a great and good human being. Hitler's spirit is universal. Not even in 100 pictures is it possible to give justice to the manifoldness of his being. In these fields too (architecture and history) Hitler is an unassailable expert. Perhaps in our time this outstanding man will be honoured and loved, but nobody will be able to measure his great depth.'

American apologist Henry Albert Phillips in *Germany Today and Tomorrow* added:

'Hitler is a modest man – and the world needs modest men. Therefore the people love him. Like every good leader, he must be an efficient follower. He makes himself the humblest disciple of himself, the severest of all disciplinarians with himself. In fact, Hitler is a modern monk, with the three knots of Poverty, Chastity and Obedience tied in his invisible girdle. A zealot among zealots. He eats no meat, drinks no wine, does not smoke. I am told he takes for himself no salary but lives privately on the incomes of his book, *Mein Kampf* ... Surplus funds he turns back to the SA. His work day consists of eighteen hours, usually, and he often falls asleep in the last hour of his work. There have been four women in his life – but only to help him along with service and money ... He once gave a lecture at Bayreuth of Wagner and *Deutsche Lieder* that astounded musical critics and revealed him as a musical scholar ... Sheer opportunism never lured him as much as the opportunity to preach his doctrines. His quality is Messianic; his spiritual trend is ascetic; his reaction is medieval ...'

Langer maintained that Hitler himself was behind this propaganda, having set out to make of himself a mythological figure. At the beginning of *Mein Kampf*, he wrote:

'In this little town on the river Inn, Bavarian by blood and Austrian by nationality, gilded by the light of German martyrdom, there lived, at the end of the '80s, my parents: the father a faithful civil servant, the mother devoting herself to the cares of a household and looking after her children with eternally the same loving kindness.'

This was a classic way of beginning a fairy tale, Langer pointed out, rather than a serious autobiography or a political treatise.

HITLER AS A GOD

Once Hitler came to power, he was personally responsible for every triumph, while his assistants were blamed for everything that did not meet with the public's approval. He became the infallible Messiah. Political rallies, particularly those at Nuremberg, took on a religious character with Hitler portrayed as a god. His portrait appeared in the window of an art shop in Berlin, surrounded by paintings of Christ. Notes appeared in the press saying: 'As he spoke, one heard God's mantle rustle through the room!' On a hillside in Odenwald, there appeared the words:

We believe in Holy Germany
Holy Germany is Hitler!
We believe in Holy Hitler!

Pictures of Hitler dressed in the silver garb of the Knights of the Grail appeared, though they were soon withdrawn. Under his portrait at the Nuremberg rally in September appeared the words: 'In the beginning was the Word ...' This is from the Gospel of St John and the quotations continued '... and the Word was with God, and the Word was God'. The mayor of Hamburg took up the theme: 'We need no priests or parsons. We communicate direct with God through Adolf Hitler. He has many Christ-like qualities.'

According to Rauschning the Party creed had become: 'We all believe, on this earth, in Adolf Hitler, our Führer, and we acknowledge that National

A Hitler Youth rally in Berlin, 1934: the immense banner proclaims, 'Youth greets the workers and the Führer'.

Socialism is the only faith that can bring salvation to our country.' One group of Rhenish Christians adopted the resolution: 'Hitler's word is God's law, the decrees and laws which represent it possess divine authority.' And Hans Kerrl, the Reichsminister for Church Affairs, said: 'There has arisen a new authority as to what Christ and Christianity really are – that is Adolf Hitler. Adolf Hitler … is the true Holy Ghost.'

This deification of Hitler was carefully managed. Anything that contradicted it was concealed. Langer conceded that it was not known how many people actually believed it. But he gave an example of some who did.

HITLER'S ABILITIES CONCERNING THE PSYCHOLOGY OF THE AVERAGE MAN

Langer listed the qualities Hitler possessed that allowed him to tap into the mind and emotions of ordinary people:

1. Full appreciation of the importance of the masses in the success of any movement

Hitler meets the Vatican ambassador in 1936: the Catholic Church has been much criticized for appeasing the Nazis.

2. Recognizing the value of winning the support of young people
3. Recognizing the role of women in advancing a new movement and that the masses have feminine characteristics
4. The ability to feel and express the deepest needs and sentiments of the average German and present opportunities for their gratification
5. The capacity to appeal to the most primitive as well as the most ideal inclinations, to arouse the basest instincts yet cloak them in nobility. Knowing that men will only combine and dedicate themselves to an ideal that will survive beyond their generation, though their zest can only be sustained with more immediate satisfactions
6. Knowing that the masses were as hungry for ideology as they were for bread
7. The ability to portray conflicting human forces in vivid imagery
8. The ability to draw on traditions and mythology to evoke unconscious emotions
9. Recognizing that political action does not occur unless emotions are involved
10. Realizing the willingness and desire of the masses to sacrifice themselves
11. Realizing the importance of artistry and drama at rallies
12. Recognizing the importance of slogans and catchphrases – because 'there is only so much room in a brain'
13. Realizing the craving of people to belong to a group that carries status
14. Appreciating the value of a hierarchical political organization that gives direct contact to every individual
15. The ability to surround himself with loyal aides
16. Realizing the importance of appearing super-efficient to win the confidence of the people

17. Realizing that little things that affect the everyday life of ordinary people build morale
18. Recognizing that most people want to be led
19. His intuition for the timing of decisions and actions
20. His firm belief in his mission and his dedication to fulfil it
21. The ability to arouse the sympathy and concern of the people
22. His ability to deny his own conscience, allowing him to act decisively without pulling his punches
23. The ability to get others to deny their conscience too
24. The ability to make use of terror
25. The capacity to learn from those who oppose him – the Communist Party, the Catholic Church, the democracies
26. His mastery of propaganda
27. His 'never-say-die' spirit and his ability to make a comeback after a setback that would have stymied most others.

RESPECT AND ADMIRATION

In part three, 'Hitler as His Associates Know Him', Langer says that although it must have been plain to those close to him that he was no superman nor the pinnacle of all virtues, he had won their respect and admiration. Sometimes he did work for days on end with no sleep and exhibit enormous powers of concentration.

They agreed with him when he said: 'I have the gift of reducing all problems to their simplest foundations ... A gift for tracing back all theories to their roots in reality.'

This meant that he was unencumbered with abstract theories and traditional points of view.

'To be sure, he never solves the entire problem this way but only the human elements involved,' said Langer. 'Since this is the part which interests him most and produces immediate results, it has been rated very highly and has won the admiration of his close associates from the earliest days of his political career.'

During periods of intense activity, Hitler was said to show great consideration to his staff, making sure that his assistants were served before him at mealtimes. He recalled details of their lives and enjoyed mimicking them. At times of friction, they had a single thought – to do what the Führer wished.

Hitler was also said to have a great command of facts and figures – the size of navies, the number of crew on each ship, the models of aircraft and the number of shots each type of machine gun fires a minute.

No other Nazi had the insight into the psychology of the masses that Hitler showed. They recognized that and admired it. His magnetic quality and his accomplishments won the allegiance of the people and robbed them of their critical faculties.

SLOPPY AND DISORDERLY

Langer quoted what were probably the truest words Goebbels ever wrote: 'The Führer does not change. He is the same now as he was when he was a boy.'

Indeed, as a boy, Hitler was far from a model student. At school his grades were 'unsatisfactory' or 'failing'. For more than a year before his mother died, he did nothing except paint a few watercolours.

After his mother died, in Vienna, he was frequently on the verge of starvation and reduced to begging in the streets. Hanisch said: 'He was never an ardent worker, was unable to get up in the morning, had difficulty getting started and seemed to be suffering from a paralysis of the will.'

When Hanisch asked what he was waiting for, Hitler replied: 'I don't know myself.'

Even those who knew him later described him as sloppy and disorderly. Kurt Ludecke, who fled Germany after the Night of the Long Knives, said: 'Hitler was always on the go but rarely on time.'

He kept irregular hours, disliking going to bed or being alone. Adjutants would have to sit up with him while he talked about trivial matters. He needed a powder to get him to sleep. Even when he went to bed, he would take with him illustrated military magazines – including American ones. Rauschning also reported that his quilt had to be folded in a particular way and his bed had to be made by a man.

PROCRASTINATION AND RAGES

His working habits were similarly irregular, ignoring the reports piled on his desk in favour of matters that interested him. He rarely attended cabinet meetings. On one occasion when he was pressured into going, he walked out and went to watch a favourite film. Generally, he preferred to discuss matters with individual members, then convey his decision to the cabinet as a whole.

Any discussion would quickly be forgotten if a newspaper appeared with a picture of him in it.

'It was almost impossible to keep Hitler concentrated on one point,' said Ludecke. 'His quick mind would run away with the talk, or his attention would be distracted by the sudden discovery of the newspaper and he would stop to read it avidly, or he would interrupt your carefully prepared report with a long speech as though you were an audience.'

Although Hitler presented himself as decisive, his staff despaired at his procrastination.

'Problems are not solved by getting fidgety,' he said, when pressed for a decision.

Frequently he hid away even from his immediate staff and, when depressed, preferred to read a book, watch a movie or play with his architectural models. He became impatient if the details of a problem were brought to him and he disliked experts. Sometimes he would leave Berlin without a word and spend his time walking at Berchtesgaden. After a lengthy period where he would brook no discussion, he would suddenly have the answer, thanks to his inner voice.

He frequently said: 'I do not look for people having clever ideas of their own but rather people who are clever in finding ways and means of carrying out my ideas.'

Langer commented:

'Instead of studying the problem as an intellectual would do he avoids it and occupies himself with other things until unconscious processes furnish him with a solution. Having the solution he then begins to look for facts which will prove that it is correct. … It is this characteristic of his thinking process which makes it difficult for ordinary people to understand Hitler or predict his future actions.'

Any challenge was met with rage, though Langer did not believe rumours that he chewed the carpet. Nevertheless, his behaviour was violent and lacking emotional control, like a spoilt child who could not have his way.

'He was an alarming sight,' said Rauschning, 'his hair dishevelled, his eyes fixed, and his face distorted and purple. I feared that he would collapse or have a stroke.'

Even minor matters could bring about this reaction if he felt that his infallibility was being challenged. He used these rages to confuse his staff and make them submissive. He could also be embarrassed easily. When a Dutch woman tried to kiss him at the Berlin Olympics, he had to leave. There were plenty of other examples of Hitler leaving without a word when the situation became embarrassing.

Tears were not uncommon, Rauschning said:

'In 1934 as in 1932 he complained of the ingratitude of the German people in the sobbing tones of a down-at-the-heel music-hall performer! A weakling who accused and sulked, appealed and implored, and retired in wounded vanity ("If the German people don't want me!") instead of acting.'

Otto Strasser reported Hitler seizing his hands – his voice 'choked with sobs, and tears flowed down his cheeks'. Awaiting Gregor Strasser, Hitler 'laid his head on the table and sobbed', said Heiden. 'Tears came to the eyes of many of those present, as they saw their Führer weeping.'

THREATS OF SUICIDE

Then there were the threats of suicide. During the Beer Hall Putsch, he said to the officials he was holding as prisoners: 'There are still five bullets in my pistol – four for the traitors and one, if things go wrong, for myself.'

After the putsch failed, he hid in Hanfstaengl's house, where he threatened to commit suicide in front of Hanfstaengl's wife. In Landsberg

Gregor Strasser, brother of Otto, was leader of the NSDAP from 1928 to 1932. He was murdered during the Night of the Long Knives.

prison, he threatened to starve himself to death. He threatened suicide again in 1930 after the death of Geli Raubal, in 1932 if Strasser split the Party, in 1933 if not appointed chancellor and in 1936 if the occupation of the Rhineland failed.

Depression had always been part of his character. After the death of his mother, Hanisch said: 'I have never seen such helpless letting down in distress.'

His comrade in World War I, Hans Mend, also said that he suffered from depression. The depression he suffered from after the death of Geli was thought to have led to a genuine suicide attempt, which he was prevented from going through with. For years after, he would go into depression during the Christmas holidays.

Even his ruthless purge of the Night of the Long Knives in 1934 depressed him, Rauschning said:

'For the present he did not give the impression of a conqueror. With his face puffed up and his features distorted, he sat opposite me as I reported to him. His eyes were dim. He did not look at me. He played with his fingers. I did not get the impression that he listened to me ... All the time it seemed to me that he wrangled with disgust, weariness and contempt and that in his thoughts he was far away ... I had heard that he was able to sleep by the hour only ... At night he wandered around restlessly. Sleeping pills did not help ... Supposedly he awoke from the short sleep in crying fits. Repeatedly he vomited. Shivering he sat in an armchair, covered with blankets ... Sometimes he wanted everything lit up and to be surrounded by people, many people; in the next moment, however, he did not want to see anybody.'

SERVILE AND SUBMISSIVE

In front of colleagues, he was not as self-confident as he believed himself to be. He was servile in the face of royalty and submissive to superior officers, always using their full title. At his trial after the failed Beer Hall Putsch, when Hitler referred to General Hans von Seeckt, head of the

Reichswehr that had put the putsch down, he stood to attention and called him 'His Excellency Herr Colonel General von Seeckt'.

He was also ill at ease with diplomats and nervous in front of newspapermen. With interviews, he insisted that questions were submitted in advance so his answers could be prepared. They usually ended with a tirade. He was terrified of intellectuals and any group that might criticize or oppose him.

Only Rudolf Hess and Julius Streicher addressed him by the familiar '*du*' (as did Röhm before he was executed during the Night of the Long Knives). Even Göring, Goebbels and Himmler had to use the more formal '*Sie*'. Apart from them only his patron Helene Bechstein and the family of Winifred Wagner used '*du*' and called him by his nickname 'Wolf'. Otherwise he had no friends.

With his staff, he would remain aloof. Unable to carry on a normal conversation, he would quickly address a listener as if they were a huge audience. Even if he tried to get closer, he insisted on doing all the talking, continually repeating stories that would already have been familiar from *Mein Kampf*.

If others sought to have a conversation in his presence, he would fall silent and pretend to be occupied with another matter. Anything he overheard that might be useful, he would repeat as if it were his own.

'If you try and tell him anything, he knows everything already,' said Röhm. 'Though he often does what we advise, he laughs in our faces at the moment, and later does the very thing as if it were all his own idea and creation. He doesn't even seem to be aware of how dishonest he is.'

He could say one thing, then the complete opposite, as if oblivious to the first statement. If anyone drew attention to the contradiction, he would fly into a rage and demand to know if he was being called a liar.

Hitler had a negligible sense of humour, confined to ribbing his colleagues. Friedelinde Wagner provided one example, given with both Goebbels and Göring present: '"You all know what a volt is and an ampere, don't you? Right. But do you know what a goebbels, a goering are? A goebbels is the amount of nonsense a man can speak in an hour and a göring is the amount of metal that can be pinned on a man's breast."'

Otherwise he resorted to mimicking.

RELATIONS WITH WOMEN

Though Hitler's name was linked with many women in the foreign press, the German public knew little of his relationships. Langer breaks them down into three categories – much older women, actresses and passing fancies and more or less enduring relationships.

In 1920, 61-year-old widow Carola Hofmann took him under her wing and Helene Bechstein, the wife of the Berlin piano manufacturer, funded Hitler during the early days of the Party. She made key introductions and said she wished he was her son. To visit him in Landsberg prison, she claimed to be his adopted mother. Hitler would sit at her feet and lay his head on her bosom, while she stroked his hair and called him 'Mein Wölfchen'. She hoped he would marry her daughter Lottie. He proposed but Lottie refused.

Viktoria von Dirksen and other wealthy female patrons also played foster mother. Goebbels' wife, Magda, eventually took over the role, supervising his household and baking for him. His older half-sister Angela also kept house for him in Munich and Berchtesgaden.

The English-born Winifred Wagner was tipped to marry Hitler after her husband, Richard Wagner's son Siegfried, died. He was a frequent visitor at her family home, staying there without a bodyguard. But nothing came of it.

Hitler enjoyed being surrounded by pretty women and got film companies to send over actresses. He liked to impress them by ordering the studios to give them better roles.

SEXUAL INDISCRETION

Another of the women who played a maternal role was the wife of his photographer, Heinrich Hoffmann. When she died, Hoffmann's home became a meeting place for homosexuals of both sexes. Hitler frequently attended parties there and a good deal of drinking was done.

Hitler became friendly with Hoffmann's daughter Henny, who Langer said was reportedly 'little more than a prostitute'. One night she got drunk and confessed her relationship with Hitler. Hoffmann was furious, but soon became official Party photographer, a position that eventually earned him a fortune.

Winifred and Wieland Wagner make polite small talk while Adolf Hitler looks like he has other things on his mind in Bayreuth, 1938.

'Among Hitler's associates, it was supposed that Hitler had committed some kind of sexual indiscretion with Henny,' said Langer, 'and had bought Hoffmann's silence by granting him these exclusive rights.'

Henny soon married Baldur von Schirach, leader of the Hitler Youth, who was thought to be homosexual. His family were against the marriage, but Hitler insisted.

Hitler then began to appear in public with Geli, daughter of his half-sister Angela, who had come to keep house for him in 1924. The relationship continued until her mysterious death in 1931.

In 1932, Hitler became interested in Hoffmann's assistant Eva Braun. The relationship developed slowly. He bought her a house and cars and she moved into the Chancellery in December 1939. It was said that he intended to marry her when the war was over. However, it was known that she had tried to kill herself twice and one of his bodyguards had committed suicide because he had fallen in love with her.

During their courtship, Hitler had continued seeing actresses at night in the Chancellery. One of them was Renate 'Rene' Müller. Hitler's peculiar relationship with her is described later in this book. The actress turned director Leni Riefenstahl also stayed at the Chancellery until the outbreak of war.

The secrecy surrounding Hitler's private life led to a great deal of speculation. Some thought that his sex life was normal, but restricted. Others thought he was above such things and nothing happened when he was alone with women. And there were those who believed he was homosexual.

This belief was rooted in the fact that many of the early Party members were homosexual. Röhm made little attempt to hide his proclivities, while Hess was widely known as 'Fraulein Anna'. Hitler said that the only criterion for membership of the Party was that they be 'unconditionally obedient and faithfully devoted to me. ... Their private lives don't concern me.'

According to Princess Stephanie von Hohenlohe, Hitler loved pornography and eagerly awaited the newest edition of Der Stürmer with its dirty stories and cartoons. He also had a large collection of nudes and

Hitler's half-sister Angela Raubal, who came to keep house for him in 1924. Her daughter Geli had a strange relationship with Hitler.

enjoyed watching 'lewd movies' in his private cinema, some of which were provided by Hoffmann.

While in later years Hitler rarely attended the opera, he often went to see a production of *The Merry Widow*, where the American actress playing the lead did a back-bending number wearing transparent butterfly wings, or sometimes nothing at all. Hitler watched through opera glasses and nudged his gauleiter, even organizing command performances for his private enjoyment.

LUXURIES

While Hitler was well known to be a vegetarian, his meals were prepared by the best chef in Germany using the finest ingredients. He would eat up to two pounds of chocolate a day and consume a large number of pastries.

Though his clothes were simple, they were made from the finest materials, procured from the best tailors, and many examples of each article of clothing were made for him. He also had a vast collection of paintings. The only thing spartan about his existence was his bedroom. It contained only a couple of straight chairs, a painted chest of drawers and a metal-framed bed with ribbons decorating the head.

According to the propaganda he was a man of great courage, but he backed down over the 'Danzig question' (the Free City of Danzig, created under the Versailles Treaty, was annexed during Germany's invasion of Poland in 1939) when opposed by three army generals. It was also said that he had decided to postpone hostilities until after the Munich Conference after discovering the crowds watching the troops marching under the windows of the Chancellery did not favour war.

When he travelled through the streets in an open car, the route was lined with troops and the crowd was packed with secret service men. He travelled in a special train with two hundred heavily armed Schutzstaffel (SS) men. When the war started, his car was armoured and had anti-aircraft guns fitted on the front and back. But the newsreels always showed him riding at the front, the only one not wearing a steel helmet.

Before the war, Hitler's house at Berchtesgaden was protected by 8 miles (13 km) of electrified fence and anti-aircraft guns and pillboxes were

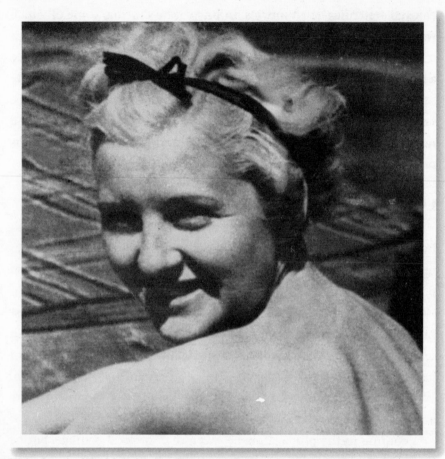

Hitler's relationship with Eva Braun took time to develop. During their courtship, Hitler continued seeing actresses in the Chancellery.

installed in the hills. The same defences were provided at Bayreuth when he paid a visit.

But while the Hitler known by his associates was very different from the Hitler known to the general public, they remained intensely loyal to the man they saw only as the Führer.

SECRETIVE

In part five, Langer considered 'Hitler as He Knows Himself'. This was hard to piece together because Hitler was very secretive. Everything was carefully pigeonholed. He would not even tell one associate what he had been discussing with another. And though he talked continually, the subjects covered almost everything under the sun – with the sole exception of himself.

'What really goes on in his mind is almost as great a mystery as his past life,' said Langer.

However, a few fragments of his past life had been unearthed and Langer found them extremely valuable as background when trying to understand his present behaviour. Fortunately, patients with behavioural patterns, tendencies and sentiments similar to those expressed by Hitler were not unknown to psychoanalysts, Langer said:

> 'From our knowledge of what goes on in the minds of these patients, together with a knowledge of their past histories, it may be possible to fill in some of the gaps and make some deductions concerning his extraordinary mode of adjustment.'

Langer first addressed the confusion surrounding Hitler's family. This was due to the fact that the name was variously spelt Hitler, Hidler, Hiedler and Huettler. His family were, after all, illiterate peasants. Hitler himself spelt his name Hittler on the first Party membership forms, while his sister was still using the Hiedler spelling. Adding to the confusion was the fact that his maternal grandmother was also named Hitler. His parents had a common ancestor – his father's grandfather and his mother's great-grandfather – in the Waldviertel, or Forest Quarter, of Lower Austria.

Like Vernon, Langer assumed that the father of Maria Schicklgruber's illegitimate son Alois was Johann Georg Hiedler, a miller's assistant. Forty years later Alois changed his name to Hitler, though it was not clear why this was done. It was assumed that it had something to do with a legacy. Langer speculated that Georg Hiedler had left Alois an inheritance along with the name. But why had he not legitimized this when he had belatedly married Alois's mother thirty-five years earlier? And why had Alois chosen an alternative spelling?

WAS HITLER A JEW?

Another line of speculation came from the police enquiry ordered by Chancellor Dollfuss. According to Langer:

'As a result of this investigation a secret document was prepared which proved that Maria Anna Schicklgruber was living in Vienna at the time she conceived. At that time she was employed as a servant in the home of Baron Rothschild. As soon as the family discovered her pregnancy she was sent back to her home in Spital where Alois was born. If it is true that one of the Rothschilds is the real father of Alois Hitler, it would make Adolf a quarter Jew.'

Langer reported further speculation that Adolf Hitler knew of the existence of this document and, to hide his Jewish roots, ordered the assassination of Dollfuss and eventually the annexation of Austria. While awaiting execution in Nuremberg, Hans Frank, Hitler's lawyer and Governor General of Poland, claimed that Hitler was worried about being blackmailed over a Jewish grandfather and had asked Frank to investigate his paternal lineage. He did so and told Hitler that his grandmother had become pregnant while working as a domestic servant in the Jewish household of Leopold Frankenberger in Graz.

FACTORS INDICATING ALOIS HITLER'S FATHER WAS NOT GEORG HIEDLER BUT A ROTHSCHILD

1. It was unlikely that a miller's assistant in a small village would have much to leave as a legacy.
2. Hiedler did not claim the boy until thirty-five years after he married the mother and she had died. (In fact, it was later discovered that Georg Hiedler was dead by then and Alois had been brought up by his uncle Johann Nepomuk Hiedler.)
3. If a legacy had been left on condition that Alois take the name Hiedler, why did he change it to Hitler?
4. The intelligence and behaviour of Alois and his two sons were out of keeping with ordinary Austrian peasant families. Their ambition and political intuition was more like that of the Rothschilds.

5. Alois left his home village at an early age to seek his fortune in Vienna where his mother had worked.
6. When working as a customs official in Braunau, according to Heiden, Alois had chosen Johann Prinz and his wife, both Jews, as Adolf's godparents, indicating he felt some kinship with Jews himself.

DOMINEERING FATHER

Alois married Hitler's mother, Klara Pölzl, in January 1885. She was already pregnant. By then Alois already had a son, Alois, and a daughter, Angela, by Franziska 'Fanni' Matzelsberger.

Their first child, Gustav, was born in May, and a daughter, Ida, was born in September of the following year. Soon after, Otto was born, but he died after a few days. Then in the winter of 1887–88 Gustav and Ida died of diphtheria within a week of each other. By the summer of 1888, Klara was pregnant again and on 20 April 1889 she gave birth to Adolf. None of this was mentioned by Hitler, who painted a very simple picture of his home life in *Mein Kampf*.

Four years after Adolf was born, his father retired as Higher Collector of Customs at the age of fifty-six. He tried his hand at farming and they moved several times, living briefly on the German side of the border. Though retired, Alois continued to wear his uniform and insisted on being addressed as Herr Oberoffizial Hitler. He spent his time drinking with friends, talking of his life as a customs official and discussing politics, and died in 1903, on his way to the tavern.

Hitler's father was described as a domineering person who was a tyrant at home. According to Hitler's nephew William Patrick Hitler, son of Hitler's half-brother Alois who had briefly married an Irish woman and lived in Liverpool, their father would beat both his wife and his children unmercifully, particularly after he had come home from the inn. On one occasion, it was said, he beat Adolf so severely he was left for dead. But having interviewed a number of villagers, Heiden contested this story.

He maintained that Hitler's home life was happy and the old man was amusing, if short-tempered.

According to Hanisch: 'Hitler heard from his father only praise of Germany and all the faults of Austria.' But Heiden said that Alois was no German nationalist and William Patrick Hitler said his grandfather was defiantly anti-German, just as his own father was.

BAD GENES

Hitler's mother Klara was said to be hard-working, energetic and conscientious. She kept her house spick and span and was devoted to her children. Dr Bloch said that she was a sweet and affectionate woman whose life centred around her children, particularly Adolf, who was her pet. She spoke highly of her husband. They lived happily together and his death was a real loss to them.

Langer had some questions about her background. One of her sister's two sons was a hunchback and had a speech impediment. Klara herself had lost three – perhaps four – children so, Langer said, 'one has grounds to question the purity of the blood'. According to Dr Bloch there was a daughter, slightly older than Adolf, who was an imbecile. This may have been Ida. A younger sister, Paula, was also said to be 'a little on the stupid side, perhaps a high-grade moron'.

'This is certainly a poor record and one is justified in suspecting some constitutional weakness,' said Langer. 'A syphilitic taint is not beyond the realm of possibility.'

HITLER'S SIBLINGS

William Patrick Hitler also told Langer about his father Alois, Adolf's older brother. According to him, Alois Jr left home early because Klara undermined his relationship with his father, who wanted to send him to technical school to train as an engineer, while his stepmother wanted their father to save the money for Adolf's education.

Alois Jr never got on with Adolf, who was spoilt by his mother. Alois had to do many of Adolf's chores and was punished by their father for the misdemeanours that Adolf had committed. They seem to have been in Vienna at the same time and since Hitler had come to power there had been practically no contact between them. What meetings they had were unpleasant, with Adolf taking a high-handed attitude. There was no mention of Alois Jr in *Mein Kampf*.

Brought up in England, William Patrick went to Germany when Hitler came to power. He obtained a lowly job in the Opel Automobile Company. Langer got the impression that he was out to blackmail his uncle. When this did not work out, he returned to England and became a British subject, then moved to America and served in the US Navy. After the war, he changed his name.

Alois, Hitler's half-brother, answers the phone in his Hamburg home; he was pestered by anonymous callers because of his name.

William Patrick Hitler, Hitler's nephew and son of Alois, signs up for the US Navy in March 1944. After the war, he changed his name.

Hitler's eldest half-sister Angela was the only sibling he kept in touch with. When his mother died, Adolf left Angela his share of the small legacy she left. She married Leo Raubal in Linz, but he died soon after. After World War I, she was the manager of the Mensa Academica Judaica, defending the Jewish students there against anti-Semitic rioters with a club.

When he was discharged from the army, Hitler visited her there after having no contact with her for ten years. She later visited him in Landsberg prison. In 1924 she moved to Munich with her daughter Geli to keep house. Later she took over the management of Berchtesgaden. They fell out in 1936 and he ordered her to leave.

Hitler's younger sister lived in poverty and seclusion in Vienna, under the name Frau Wolff. He had little contact with her, though it was thought that he sent her a small allowance.

LIFE AS A CHILD

Langer then tried to imagine what life was like for Hitler as a child. His father was twenty-three years older than his mother. She had been his foster-daughter and she had witnessed his life with his wives and mistresses. It can hardly have been a romantic marriage as he spent much of his time at the tavern.

His mother had lost three or four older children, so Adolf became the centre of her life. Then, when he was five, a terrible thing happened – she had another child, his younger brother Edmund. His position had been usurped. Then a baby sister was born. He was sent off to school and had to look after himself. But then, when he was eleven, his brother died, Paula was hidden away and, again, Adolf became the apple of his mother's eye. Langer believed that this extraordinary sequence of events left its mark on Hitler's immature personality.

He first went to school at the age of six and although they kept moving from place to place he seems to have done rather well. At eight, he attended a Benedictine Monastery in Lambach. There he developed an ambition to become an abbot, but was expelled for smoking in the gardens. Even so, at Volksschule, he continued to get high marks.

He entered Realschule (secondary school) in Linz in 1900. This was the year his younger brother died. Suddenly his marks were poor and he had

Paula Wolff, Hitler's youngest sister, after her arrest by US troops in May 1945. She was six years younger than Adolf.

to retake a grade. His father died when he was fourteen and he changed schools again. He only excelled in drawing and gymnastics, failing in both German and history.

According to Hitler's own account, he was at odds with his father over his ambition to become an artist, so deliberately failed at all subjects that did not help him towards that goal – with the exception of history, which he said fascinated him. This was not borne out by his report cards. Langer said: 'A better diagnosis would be that he was outstanding in those subjects which did not require any preparation or thought while in those that required application he was sadly lacking.'

Hitler was much taken with Karl May's Wild West stories. He took bowie knives and hatchets to school and tried to get others to play Indians, with him as their leader, but the other boys were not greatly impressed.

In his twelfth year, he was found guilty of *Sittlichkeitsvergehen* – 'moral offences'. Dr Bloch recalled a teacher telling him about this and felt certain that it involved a little girl. He narrowly escaped being expelled and changed schools the following year. At sixteen, he stopped going to school altogether, though Dr Bloch insisted that there was nothing wrong with him.

Though his mother's income was modest, Hitler made no attempt to find work. Otherwise he dabbled in art. Taking long walks in the hills, ostensibly to paint, he was seen delivering speeches to the landscape.

END OF FAMILY LIFE

Hitler's mother died on 21 December 1907, shortly after his failure to enter the Academy of Fine Arts in Vienna, and was buried on Christmas Eve. He sketched her on her deathbed. According to Dr Bloch, Hitler was completely broken.

'In all my career I have never seen anyone so prostrate with grief,' he said.

After the funeral he stood for a long time beside the grave after the others had left and expressed his feelings to no one.

The family broke up as Hitler moved to Vienna in emulation of his father. He tried to enter the Academy of Fine Arts a second time but was not allowed to sit the entrance examination again. Langer thought this would have been a greater shock than his failure to pass the examination the previous year. The director told him that his talents lay in architecture, but he was refused entrance to the School of Architecture because he had not finished Realschule.

With his grandiose dreams thwarted, he was forced to support himself with manual labour. But he felt himself to be a cut above the other working men and sat apart from them when eating lunch. They tried to convert him to Marxism, but at school in Linz he had become an ardent German nationalist. It was all the more galling that they knew more than he did and he was unable to answer their arguments.

To justify his position, he began reading pamphlets and attending political meetings. This only succeeded in antagonizing his fellow workers and he was run off the job. On the verge of starvation he found odd jobs, carrying luggage, shovelling snow and running errands, though he spent most of his time begging or standing in breadlines.

THE FLOPHOUSE

Thrown out of his room when he could not pay the rent, the twenty-year-old Hitler was forced to resort to a flophouse. There he met Reinhold Hanisch, who was in much the same predicament. He recalled that Hitler was a sorry sight; badly dressed with a full black beard and a haggard look.

Hitler did not hate Jews at the time. There were a number of Jews living in Männerheim Brigittenau hostel with whom he was on excellent terms. Most of his paintings were sold to Jewish dealers. He even expressed his admiration for Rothschild for sticking to his religion, even though this meant he could not enter court.

Back in Linz, Dr Bloch, a Jew, received two postcards from Hitler expressing his gratitude. Hanisch said: 'Hitler at that time looked very Jewish, so that I often joked with him that he must be of Jewish blood, since such a large beard rarely grows on a Christian's chin. Also he had big feet, as a desert wanderer must have.'

Later they fell out.

Hanfstaengl said homosexual men frequented the hostel, looking for companions. It was also said that on the police record Hitler was listed as a sexual pervert, though it gave no details of offences. Another source said that the Viennese police also had a charge for theft on file and that he fled to Munich in 1912 to avoid arrest. His older brother Alois was in Vienna at the time. He had two convictions for theft and Adolf may have taken to crime with him. Hanisch said he spent much of his time thinking up shady schemes.

'He proposed to fill old tin-cans with paste and sell them to shopkeepers, the paste to be smeared on windowpanes to keep them from freezing in winter. It should be sold ... in the summer, when it couldn't be tried out. I told him it wouldn't work because the merchants would just say, come back in the winter ... Hitler answered that one must possess a talent for oratory.'

WHY HITLER WANTED TO BE AN ARTIST

Langer enumerated a number of factors:

1. The rejection of his father as a role model
2. His antipathy towards any career that required thinking
3. His anal tendencies that found an outlet of expression in smearing
4. His passive, feminine tendencies
5. His masochistic tendencies and his desire to be dominated by a strong masculine figure

A watercolour by Adolf Hitler dating from 1910: his style was a little laboured and old-fashioned.

As Hitler could rarely be persuaded to do any work, he spent a great deal of time reading political pamphlets and newspapers and delivering speeches to the other inmates of the hostel. He became a great admirer of the rabble-rousing mayor Karl Lueger and Georg Ritter von Schönerer, the Austrian pan-German nationalist and anti-Semite. Anti-Semitism crept into Hitler's speech and despite a good deal of ridicule he talked of starting a new political party.

He said that he left for Munich to get away from the mixture of people, particularly the Jews, and that Vienna, for him, was a symbol of incest. As far as Hitler was concerned, his five years of poverty and inaction there were not wasted.

'In a few years I built a foundation of knowledge from which I still draw nourishment today,' he wrote in *Mein Kampf*. 'At that time I formed an image of the world and a view of life which became the granite foundations for my actions.'

THE GREAT WAR

Things were not much better for him in Munich. He earned a little money painting posters and postcards, and occasionally houses. Early in 1913, he returned to Salzburg to report for duty in the Austrian army but was rejected as unfit. Back in Munich he spent his time reading the newspapers. Then came the Great War, of which he wrote:

> 'The struggle of the year 1914 was not forced on the masses – no, by the living God – it was desired by the whole people. To me those hours seemed like a release from the painful feelings of my youth. Even today I am not ashamed to say that, overpowered by stormy enthusiasm, I fell down on my knees and thanked Heaven from an overflowing heart for granting me the good fortune of being permitted to live at this time.'

He joined a Bavarian regiment and became an orderly as well as a runner. On 7 October 1917, he was wounded by a piece of shrapnel. Soon discharged from hospital, he was sent back to Munich, but after two days he wrote to his commanding officer asking to be recalled. Then on 14 October 1918 he was gassed. Blinded and having lost his voice, he was sent to hospital in Pasewalk.

Langer was puzzled why Hitler did not rise above the rank of lance corporal and why the story of how he won the Iron Cross, First Class did not appear in the regimental history.

'The Nazi propaganda agencies have not helped clarify the situation,' he said, noting that numerous different versions of the story had appeared in the German press, even though they purported to print facsimiles of the citation. Strasser reckoned that at the end of the war Regimental Headquarters gave out their remaining Iron Crosses willy-nilly. Hitler's regimental sergeant-major, Max Amann, later became head of the Nazi Eher Verlag, one of the most lucrative positions in the Nazi hierarchy.

The only published explanation for his lack of promotion was that one of his officers said it was not possible to make a non-commissioned officer 'out of that neurotic fellow, Hitler'. But Rauschning claimed a Nazi official had told him he had seen Hitler's military record, which contained the verdict of a court martial finding Hitler guilty of pederastic practices with an officer. That was why he had never been promoted. Rauschning also claimed that Hitler had been convicted of pederasty in Munich too, though no evidence of these offences had come to light. For Langer this remained a mystery, as many informants had said that Hitler was courageous and never dodged dangerous assignments. Indeed he readily volunteered.

Langer also noted that after living in flophouses and standing on breadlines, in the army he had become a member of a recognized and respected institution.

'For the first time since his mother died he really did belong to a group of people,' Langer said. 'Not only did this provide him with a sense of pride and security but at last he had achieved his great ambition, to be one with the German nation.'

Instead of wearing the cast-offs of Jews and other charitable people he had a uniform, which he spent so much time cleaning when he came back from an assignment that he became the joke of the regiment.

Langer remarked that this was 'quite a remarkable change for one who for almost seven years refused to exert himself just a little in order to pull

A portrait of Hitler from 1925 which shows him in *lederhosen* and Nazi uniform; he is bulky because he's wearing a bulletproof vest.

himself out of the pitiful conditions in which he lived among the dregs of society'.

However, after the Armistice, he risked falling back into the same position.

FIRST POLITICAL ACTIVITY

With nowhere to go, Hitler managed to stay on with the army reserve stationed at Traunstein, where he suffered a deep depression. There was unrest among the troops and every tenth man in the barracks was shot, but it appeared that Hitler had been singled out beforehand and told to stand to one side. He then denounced others for communist activities. It seemed that he had been spying on his comrades, thereby assigning them to the executioner.

'This was my first more or less purely political activity,' he said in *Mein Kampf*.

The army then decided to give its soldiers a political education and Hitler was appointed education officer. He was picked out for his talent as a speaker and, with growing confidence, was soon addressing large groups.

'He was on his way to becoming a politician,' said Langer in his report. 'From here on his career is a matter of history and need not be reviewed here.'

The details he had given up to that point, he said, were the foundations of Hitler's character. Whatever he tried later was merely superstructure.

CHAPTER 6
The Diagnosis

Langer said that the four psychoanalysts who had studied
the material with him agreed that Hitler was 'an hysteric
bordering on schizophrenia and not a paranoiac as is
so frequently supposed'. That meant he was not insane,
but neurotic. He had not completely lost contact with the
world and was striving to make some kind of psychological
adjustment to fit into his social group. It also meant
that there was still a moral component to his character
no matter how deeply buried or seriously distorted.

After making that diagnosis, they were in a position to make some
deductions about his conscious mental processes. They supposed
that Hitler was not happy, but harassed by fears, anxieties, doubts,
misgivings, uncertainties, condemnations and feelings of loneliness and
guilt. From their experience with other hysterics, they guessed that he
was pulled this way and that by conflicting and contradictory impulses
in a 'battle-royal'.

Reviewing the evidence from those close to Hitler, Langer drew the
impression that he was two people inhabiting the same body. One was
soft, sentimental and indecisive, with little drive, who needed to be
amused and looked after. This was evidenced by the seven years from the
death of his mother until the outbreak of war, when he did nothing unless
driven to do so by hunger. The same process pertained afterwards, when
he would procrastinate until the situation became dangerous and he was
forced to take action. Once the crisis was averted he slipped back into

inertia. The other was hard, cruel and decisive, with abundant energy, who would pursue any goal regardless of cost.

One wept over the death of a canary, could not bring himself to fire an assistant and spent his evenings watching movies or going to cabarets. The other cried 'Heads will roll' in open court, could order the murder of hundreds including his best friends, said with conviction 'There will be no peace until a body hangs from every lamppost' and worked for days on end, often without sleep, making plans that would affect the destiny of nations.

JEKYLL AND HYDE

This Jekyll and Hyde split was common in hysterics and psychopaths, Langer said. The conflict was seen in action by American diplomat William Russell when an elaborate commemoration was laid on for Germans that had died when a battleship was bombed. As Hitler spoke to the first widow in the reception line, her ten-year-old son began to cry and Hitler patted him on the head. But before he could utter a word to the next in line, he was overcome. He sprinted to his car and drove away, abandoning all the arrangements.

Ludecke said: 'There were times when he gave an impression of unhappiness, of loneliness, of inward searching ... But in a moment, he would turn again to whatever frenzied task with the swift command of a man born for action.'

While Rauschning observed: 'Almost anything might suddenly inflame his wrath and hatred ... But equally, the transition from anger to sentimentality or enthusiasm might be quite sudden.'

His eyes could be soft and dreamy then suddenly flash and harden, and the slightest obstacle could make him scream with rage or burst into tears. Heiden contrasted the two sides of his nature as 'Hitler' and the 'Führer'.

Langer did not find a complete dissociation of the two personalities, beyond voluntary control, as he was able to flip between them almost at will. One example was his speechmaking – he became nervous and insecure as little 'Hitler', but once he got a feel for the audience he transformed into the great 'Führer'. He also made that transformation

Hitler poses aboard a ferry on the Baltic in 1921; at this time, he was the Nazis' prize asset and had just taken over leadership of the Party.

when making a decision, changing from the dithering Hitler into the resolute Führer.

'Before Hitler can act, he must lash himself out of lethargy and doubts into a frenzy,' said Rauschning.

Hitler could play the role of 'Führer' to perfection. But the transformation meant that the 'Führer' could contradict what 'Hitler' had said minutes earlier. Suddenly, he was clear-sighted and decisive. Having put away all moral considerations, he could order executions or the destruction of cities without hesitation. This would have been impossible for 'Hitler'.

Hitler liked to pretend that the 'Führer' was his true self, but it was artifice – an exaggerated and distorted conception of masculinity as he saw it. It was what he would have liked to be. In reality, like other hysterics, Hitler was covering up and compensating for tendencies within himself that he despised.

'The great difference between Hitler and other psychopaths is that he managed to convince millions of other people that the image is really

Hitler asleep on a deckchair during a rare, unguarded moment in 1930. His niece Geli Raubal looks on with amusement.

himself,' said Langer. 'The more he was able to convince them, the more he became convinced of it himself.'

DESPICABLE FELLOW

Langer believed that he had fallen in love with the image he had created and did his utmost to forget that behind it lay another Hitler who was a despicable fellow. But his ability to convince others saved him from insanity. Nevertheless, underneath he was a bundle of secret fears and anxieties which, though he rationalized or displaced them, continued to haunt him.

Terrified of cancer, he refused the assurance of doctors. He was afraid of being poisoned, assassinated, growing ill, growing fat, treason, losing his mystical guidance, premature death, leaving his mission unfulfilled. He no longer trusted the Gestapo and generals had to surrender their swords before entering his presence.

Sleep no longer offered sanctuary from such fears and his terror of betrayal led to a narrowing of his world. Even before the outbreak of World War II, he told a member of staff at Berchtesgaden: 'I am the loneliest man in the world.'

Hitler did not see this as a weakness, but rather confirmation of his importance. The smaller his personal world became, the more he extended his physical domain. Meanwhile, he inflated his image with plans of huge buildings and memorials, tangible symbols of his greatness. But no matter what he achieved, it was never enough to convince him that things were what he wanted them to be.

The insecurity would not go away because the security he sought was not outside but within himself and should have been gained by conquering unsocial impulses when he was young. These insecurities gnawed away at his psyche like termites, making the superstructure he had built above ever shakier.

PERVERSION

Some psychopaths manage to repress their unsocial impulses completely, but Hitler did not. Langer dismissed the theories that Hitler was a chronic masturbator, satisfied by voyeurism, completely impotent or homosexual.

'His perversion has quite a different nature, which few have guessed,' Langer said. 'It is an extreme form of masochism in which the individual derives sexual gratification from the act of having a woman urinate or defecate on him.'

Otto Strasser explained that this was what had happened with Geli.

'Hitler made her undress. He would then lie on the floor. She would have to squat on his face where he could examine her at close quarters and this made him very excited.

'It was of the utmost importance to Hitler that Geli squat over him in such a way as he could see everything.

'When the excitement reached its peak, he demanded that she urinate on him and that gave him sexual pleasure. Geli said the whole performance was extremely disgusting to her and it gave her no gratification.'

Strasser had heard such things before from Henriette 'Henny' Hoffmann, but had dismissed them as hysterical ravings. However, the chambermaids who cleaned up Geli's bedroom complained of the 'very strange and unspeakable' things that had been going on there. Geli also told a girlfriend that Hitler was 'a monster – you would never believe the things he makes me do'.

All five of the psychoanalysts who collaborated on the study agreed with this conclusion. Meanwhile, Hitler had to struggle both with the fear of being found out and guilt.

EARLY LIFE

Langer concluded his report with 'Part V: Psychological Analysis and Reconstruction'. In it, he again rues the poverty of material he had to work with. So he turned to what he called Sigmund Freud's 'earliest and greatest contribution ... his discovery of the importance of the first years of a child's life in shaping his future character'. Hitler's early life, he found, was a closely guarded secret. In *Mein Kampf* he had portrayed his home life as an idyll. But if that was really the case, why would he go to such lengths to conceal it?

Little more was said about his mother. His brothers and sisters were not mentioned and only a few close associates knew of his half-sister Angela.

'We become even more suspicious when we find that not a single patient manifesting Hitler's character traits has grown up in such a well-ordered and peaceful home environment,' said Langer.

However, in *Mein Kampf* Hitler did give a description of a child's life in a lower-class family:

> 'Among the five children there is a boy, let us say, of three ... When the parents fight almost daily, their brutality leaves nothing to the imagination; then the results of such visual education must slowly but inevitably become apparent to the little one. Those who are not familiar with such conditions can hardly imagine the results, especially when the mutual differences express themselves in the form of brutal attacks on the part of the father towards the mother or to assaults due to drunkenness. The poor little boy at the age of six senses things which would make even a grown-up person shudder.'

Coincidentally, there were five children in Hitler's household and his father drank heavily in the village tavern. It was not beyond the bounds of possibility that Hitler was describing his own childhood.

He continued:

> '... things end badly indeed when the man from the very start goes his own way and the wife, for the sake of the children stands up against him. Quarrelling and nagging set in, and in the same measure in which the husband becomes estranged from his wife, he becomes familiar with alcohol. ... When he finally comes home ... drunk and brutal, but always without a last cent or penny, then God have mercy on the scenes which follow. I witnessed all of this personally in hundreds of scenes and at the beginning with both disgust and indignation.'

During the course of his life, Hitler did not have a single intimate friend, so the household he described could only be his own.

He then offered an explanation of much of his later behaviour:

> 'The other things the little fellow hears at home do not tend to
> further his respect for his surroundings. Not a single good shred
> is left for humanity, not a single institution is left unattacked;
> starting with the teacher, up to the head of the State, be it religion,
> or morality as such, be it the State or society, no matter which,
> everything is pulled down in the nastiest manner into the filth of
> a depraved mentality.'

But when he was sober, his father stood on his dignity and prided himself
on his rank in the civil service. Even at home he insisted on being called
'*Herr Vater*'. In other words, Hitler's father was a contradictory figure
for a young boy to emulate – on one hand the soul of dignity, propriety,
sternness and justice; on the other brutal, unjust, inconsiderate and a
violent bully.

The young Hitler could never predict how his father would behave. This
left him confused and insecure. The person who was supposed to give
him love, support and a feeling of security filled him with uncertainty,
uneasiness and anxiety. And this confusion was projected on to the world
outside the home too.

ROLE MODELS

As a child, Hitler must have searched for a strong masculine figure he
could respect and emulate. There was evidence that he tried to see some
of his teachers in this way, but failed. Later he looked to figures in history
– Julius Caesar, Napoleon, Frederick the Great. Then in Vienna, Hitler
took the anti-Semites Schönerer and Lueger as his models.

The army then substituted for a home life and he was excessively
respectful to officers. After the war, he continued to do whatever they
asked and when they singled him out for special propaganda work he
was overjoyed.

Hitler then looked upon himself as the 'drummer-boy' heralding the
coming of the great leader. He looked up to Gustav Ritter von Kahr,
who ousted the socialist administration after the fall of the Bavarian

Soviet Republic. Then he turned to Erich Ludendorff, the German general who took a leading role in the Beer Hall Putsch. Finally there was Paul von Hindenburg, who was president when Hitler first came to power as chancellor.

Each in turn was discarded and treated in despicable fashion once he noticed their shortcomings. This was typical of neurotic people like Hitler who, in later life, still craved guidance from an older man. Once they reached maturity, only a superman who was perfect in every respect would do. They would seek out people of ever higher status, then reject them when they failed to live up to expectations. Consequently, Hitler himself had to become the Führer – the Leader – his own role model.

LIBIDINAL ATTACHMENT

Then there was Hitler's strong bond with his mother. Langer called this a 'libidinal attachment' as she received little affection from her elderly husband. Undoubtedly young Adolf used temper tantrums to get his own

Administrator of Upper Bavaria, Gustav Ritter von Kahr was one of the powerful men Hitler most looked up to when he was young.

way. Langer also believed that she condoned behaviour that his father would disapprove of, particularly during his father's absences. Life with his mother must have been a 'veritable paradise' – until his father came home.

His libidinal attachment to his mother and his father's objectionable behaviour must have developed his Oedipus complex to an extraordinary degree, Langer said. No doubt Hitler fantasized about getting rid of his father. And when his sickly younger brother was born, depriving Adolf of his mother's attention, he would have fantasized about getting rid of him too.

Langer concluded that:

> 'The other factor which served to intensify these feelings was the fact that as a child he must have discovered his parents during intercourse. An examination of the data makes this conclusion almost inescapable and from our knowledge of his father's character and past history it is not at all improbable.'

Langer assumed that on this occasion his feelings would be very mixed. While he would be indignant over what he would consider his father's brutal assault, he would also be indignant with his mother for submitting so willingly. And he would be indignant with himself for being powerless to intervene. He lost all respect for women and never put himself in their hands again – except possibly in the case of Geli Raubal, and that ended in disaster.

Langer believed that Hitler unconsciously transferred all the emotions he had once felt for his mother to Germany – which, having only recently been united, was also young and vigorous. He was also shut off from Germany, as he had become shut off from his mother, though he secretly wanted to be with her. In his writings and speeches, Germany became his ideal mother.

Austria, like his father, was old and decayed, and Hitler unconsciously transferred his hatred of his father to the Austrian state. His emotions could then be articulated symbolically. In *Mein Kampf*, he talked frequently of his love of Germany and seeking the destruction of Austria. In the *Anschluss*, unconsciously, he was not dealing with nations comprising millions of people, but trying to resolve his personal conflicts and rectify the injustices of his childhood.

HYSTERICAL SYMPTOMS

When World War I broke out, Hitler found he could fight for his symbolic mother, prove his manhood and be accepted by her. But at the end of the war, he found that his symbolic mother was going to be degraded as his real mother had been degraded in his childhood.

Although he had been exposed to mustard gas, his symptoms did not correspond to a genuine case of gassing when he was in hospital. The doctor who treated him used his case as an illustration of hysterical symptoms in the course he taught in medical school after the war. For Langer, Hitler was reliving the experience of discovering his parents in the act of intercourse. He refused to believe what he saw with his eyes and the experience left him speechless. Later, he repeatedly talked of Germany being raped.

It was while he was blind and mute in hospital that Hitler had the vision that he would liberate Germany from her bondage and make her great again.

'From an analysis of many other cases, we know that such convictions never result from an adult experience alone,' said Langer. 'In order to carry conviction they must reawaken earlier beliefs which have their roots far back in childhood.'

It was not unusual for a child to believe that he was a special creation, destined to do great things before he died. But in Hitler's case this would have been greatly reinforced by the deaths of two, or possibly three, siblings before his birth and his mother's special concern for him. Then came the death of his younger brother, Edmund. This gave him good reason to believe that he was the 'chosen one'. Surviving the war, when so many didn't, once again convinced him that he was under divine protection.

MESSIAH COMPLEX

Langer explored Hitler's 'messiah complex' further. He noted that it was not uncommon for children that were spoilt at an early age and had a strong bond with their mother to question their paternity. This was most marked in the eldest child when the father was much older than the mother.

When at his Benedictine school Hitler expressed an ambition to become a priest or an abbot. Then, in Vienna, he grew a Christ-like beard. He believed that some extra-natural power guided him and spoke through him. He was to be the saviour of Germany and become a competitor to Christ in the affections of the German people.

While his siblings had died, he had lived. He had even survived the murderous assaults of his father. Surely he was immortal. But as he approached an age when a man might reasonably expect to die, the fear of death could no longer be completely repressed. Most people consoled themselves with a religion that promised an afterlife, or with the thought that they would go on living through their children. Neither of these options was open to Hitler. He had to go on living through the German people for a thousand years at least, ousting Christ and taking his place.

Nevertheless, the fear of death continued to plague him, either through assassination or cancer, his most irrational fear. But then his mother had died after an operation for breast cancer.

With the war turning against him, it became increasingly difficult for him to believe that he could cheat death and achieve immortality, but he would keep on trying as long as a ray of hope remained. The danger was that if he could not achieve immortality as the Great Redeemer, Langer said, he would seek to live on in the minds of the German people as the Great Destroyer.

In a conversation with Rauschning, Hitler had said: 'We shall not capitulate – no, never. We may be destroyed, but if we are, we shall drag a world with us – a world in flames.'

For Hitler, it was to be immortality at any price, an ambition he has perhaps achieved.

SYPHILOPHOBIA

Next, Langer considered Hitler's sexual development. He assumed that as his mother was excessively clean and tidy, she would have employed rather stringent methods during toilet training.

'This usually results in a residual tension in this area and is regarded by the child as a severe frustration which arouses feelings of hostility. This facilitates an alliance with his infantile aggression which finds an avenue for expression through anal activities and fantasies. These usually centre around soiling, humiliation and destruction, and form the basis of a sadistic character.'

The experience would have been all the more intense for Hitler because he had been spoilt in early life and was unused to dealing with minor frustrations – as, indeed, he was in later life. The images he used in his speeches and writing often involved dung, dirt and smell.

His libidinal development progressed to the genital stage with his Oedipus complex reaching its greatest intensity just when his mother was pregnant again. If his secret desires towards his mother were discovered, Hitler feared his father would castrate him, Langer believed. This fear expressed itself in later life as syphilophobia. In *Mein Kampf,* Hitler returned to the subject of syphilis repeatedly and devoted almost an entire chapter to it.

Langer explained:

'In almost all cases we find that a fear of this sort is rooted in a fear of genital injury during childhood. In many cases this fear was so overpowering that the child abandoned his genital sexuality entirely and regressed to earlier stages of libidinal development.'

In later life, fear of syphilis was given as an excuse to avoid intercourse. During his early adult life, he showed no interest in women. Even when he came to power, his relationships with women appeared asexual, leading some observers to conclude that he had suffered some injury to his genitals during the war, or that he was homosexual. Langer dismissed this conjecture.

In such cases, Langer said, the eyes can become a substitute sexual organ. Those who met him commented on his eyes, which seemed to bore through them. Hitler enjoyed striptease and watching nude dancing. Strippers were often invited to the Brown House, the Nazi headquarters in Munich. He also invited girls to Berchtesgaden to pose nude. Graphic

A brooding figure, Hitler looks out over the Obersalzberg Mountains from the Berghof residence, 1938.

pictures of nudes decorated his walls and he took a particular delight in a collection of pornographic photographs Hoffmann had prepared for him.

The buttocks and faeces were also sexualized. His mouth too was an erogenous zone, consuming huge quantities of sweets, cakes, pastries and whipped cream. His refusal to smoke, drink beer or eat meat suggested unconscious inhibitions in that area. He also had a pathological fear of poison and washed his mouth obsessively, as if trying to get rid of something disgusting. Langer also pointed out that his hysterical attack at the end of World War I involved both blindness and mutism – both the eyes and the mouth.

The effect of his mother's pregnancy and his consequent estrangement from her resulted in an idealization of love without a sexual component. It also set up a barrier against intimate relations with others, particularly women. He tried to overcome that with Geli, with tragic results, and after that he gave up intimate relations with either men or women. Instead, he cut himself off from the world and fixated on Germany. It was a love that had no sexual dimension.

His mother's pregnancy would also have piqued his curiosity. Most children wonder how the baby got into a woman's belly and how it got out. Even when a child sees a couple having sex, they rarely associate it with any ensuing pregnancy. In a child's limited experience, things get to the belly via the mouth and come out via the anus.

'This curiosity laid the foundation for his strange perversion which brought all three of his sexualized zones into play,' said Langer. This fits in with Geli's description of her sexual experiences with Hitler, when he would get her to squat over him in such a way that he risked getting urine or faeces in his mouth.

RETURN TO THE WOMB

When home life was harsh, a child often fantasized about returning to the womb. But there, the child believed, there would be nothing to eat or drink except faeces and urine. This put off most children, but in psychotics the fantasy lingered.

As evidence for Hitler's desire to return to the womb, Langer cited the Kehlstein or Eagle's Nest near Berchtesgaden, which many had said no one but a madman would conceive of, let alone build. It was approached by a long road cut through the rock. The entrance was heavily guarded. After passing through the heavy door, there was a long passage. At the top of a vertical shaft through the rock was a circular room. With windows all around, it seemed to hang in space and was bathed in an ethereal light that made a visitor wonder whether they were awake or dreaming.

'If one were asked to plan something which represented a return to the womb, one could not possibly surpass the Kehlstein,' said Langer. 'It is also significant that Hitler often retires to this strange place to await instructions concerning the course he is to pursue.'

Langer traced Hitler's vegetarianism and abstention from alcohol to the same source.

'In terms of unconscious symbolism meat is almost synonymous with faeces and beer with urine,' he said.

This found political expression too. Hitler ascribed the decay of civilization to constipation – faeces stuck in the gastro-intestinal tract. This was caused by excessive beer drinking and, one day, he said, nations would give up feeding on dead animals. However, one informant told Langer that Hitler only became a real vegetarian after the death of Geli.

'In clinical practice, one almost invariably finds compulsive vegetarianism setting in after the death of a loved object,' Langer said.

GROVELLING BEHAVIOUR

Langer saw Hitler's perversion as a compromise between psychotic tendencies to eat faeces and drink urine and living a normal, socially adjusted life.

'We must not suppose that Hitler gratifies his strange perversion frequently. Patients of this type rarely do and in Hitler's case it is highly probable that he has permitted himself to go this far only with his niece, Geli.'

As the practice of this perversion represented the lowest depths of degradation, it would only arise when he had established a strong love relationship and sexuality made its demands. Otherwise he would content himself with less degrading activities.

Here Langer cited the actress Renate Müller, who had spent an evening in the Chancellery. The following morning, her director asked her what was troubling her. She said she was sure that Hitler was going to have sex with her. They both undressed, apparently for bed, when Hitler fell to the floor and begged her to kick him. She refused, but he pleaded with her. Grovelling in an agonizing fashion, he said he was unworthy and accused himself of all sorts of things. The scene was unbearable and eventually she gave way and kicked him. This excited him and he begged for more, saying he was unworthy to be in the same room as her. As she continued kicking him, he grew more and more excited.

Shortly afterwards she committed suicide, though it has also been alleged that she was murdered by the Gestapo.

A number of informants said that when Hitler liked a girl he would grovel at her feet. He would often tell women that he was unworthy.

Langer explains Hitler's behaviour:

'It is now clear that the only way in which Hitler can control these copraphagic tendencies or their milder manifestations is to isolate himself from any intimate relationship in which warm feelings of affection or love might assert themselves. As soon as such feelings are aroused, he feels compelled to degrade himself in the eyes of the loved object and eat their dirt figuratively, if not literally.'

These tendencies disgusted Hitler just as much as anyone else. When they got out of control, he despised himself and condemned himself for his weakness.

PASSIVE ROLE

Hitler always played the passive role and seemed to have identified with his mother, who must have been a masochist or she would not have endured such brutal treatment from her husband. This would have been easy for him as he had a large feminine component in his physical make-up. It would have resulted in the passive, sentimental and submissive component of his character.

Hanfstaengl said that he had shown Hitler's handwriting to Carl Jung, who immediately identified it as typically feminine. Washing the

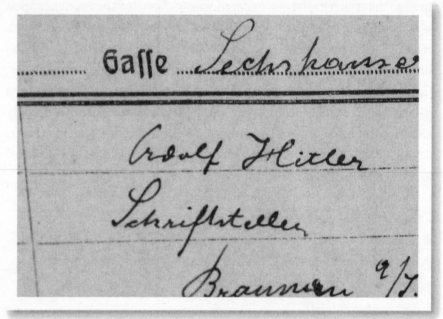

Portion of a 1909 police document in Hitler's handwriting recording a new address; he had to move a month later because he was broke.

clothes of the officers during the war and his fear of cancer were both manifestations of his identification with his mother. Langer noted that this might be common in Germany and might prove valuable to their psychological warfare programme.

Boys who identify with their mothers are often carried in the direction of 'passive homosexuality'. For years, it was thought that Hitler was homosexual. Rauschning said that he had met two boys who said they were Hitler's homosexual partners. He also reported conversations with Albert Förster, Gauleiter of Danzig, about Hitler's impotence in heterosexual relations. Hitler also called Förster 'Bubi', a nickname often adopted by homosexuals for their partners. He was clearly more at ease around homosexuals, but that may have been because they were also social outcasts and often thought they were special, the forerunner of a new social order.

Already on the fringes of society, homosexuals were easy converts to any new philosophy that might improve their lot. Many joined the early Nazi Party. Hitler derived pleasure from looking at men's bodies and

Strasser said his personal bodyguard was 100 per cent homosexual. He also took a womanly attitude towards the Hitler Youth.

Langer thought it was possible that Hitler had participated in a homosexual relationship at some time in his life. There was a strong tendency in that direction, though his nightmares suggested that he had repressed it. However, people suffering from his perversion did indulge in homosexual practices in the hope of gratification.

'Even this perversion would be more acceptable to them than the one with which they are afflicted,' said Langer.

GERMAN NATIONALISM

At school, Hitler pretended to be a leader. In fact, he was not well liked by the other boys and teachers found him lazy, unco-operative and a troublemaker. There was only one teacher he got on with; Dr Leopold Pötsch, a fervid German nationalist.

'It was probably during this period that he discovered a resemblance between the young state of Germany and his mother, and between the old Austrian monarchy and his father,' Langer said.

Athletes drawn from the ranks of storm troopers, the SS Guard and Hitler Youth salute their leader at the Germanic Games, 1938.

He joined a nationalist students' group, declaring – psychologically – his love of his mother and calling for the death of his father. This again put him at odds with his father, who was anti-German. But his father then fell dead in the street. To the young Adolf this must have appeared to be another mysterious fulfilment of a death wish – the first being the death of his brother Edmund – perhaps accompanied by some guilt.

He changed schools, but his performance did not improve. It was then, he claimed, that a doctor told him he had a disease from which he would not recover and he retired to bed to be pampered by his mother, who must surely have needed a bread-winner in the house.

When his mother died, Hitler followed in his father's footsteps and went to seek his fortune in Vienna, but did not do well at it and found himself among the dregs of society. In 1913 he moved to Munich, but did not do much better there.

THE CHOSEN ONE

Then along came World War I, giving him an opportunity to redeem his mother and himself. Activity replaced passivity. Instead of being an outcast, he mixed on equal terms with others and the army gave him a chance to assume a masculine role.

Langer assumed that Hitler's hysterical reaction to Germany's defeat was similar to that which he had experienced when, as a child, he had discovered his parents having sexual intercourse.

'It seems logical to suppose that, at that time, he felt his mother as being defiled before his eyes, but in view of his father's power and brutality he felt himself utterly helpless to redeem her honour or to save her from future assaults. If this is true, we would expect that he swore secret vengeance against his father … Now the same thing was happening again but instead of his real mother it was his ideal mother, Germany, who was being betrayed, corrupted and humiliated and again he was unable to come to her rescue.'

Lying helplessly in a hospital bed, Langer thought that Hitler also feared homosexual rape, something he both consciously wished for and was

Armed demonstrators head towards the newspaper district of Berlin on
5 January 1919; following World War I, Germany seethed with discontent.

repelled by. Meanwhile, Germany was being poisoned with propaganda.

'There is considerable evidence to show that as a child he believed that the man, during intercourse, injected poison into the woman which gradually destroyed her from within and finally brought about her death,' said Langer, who also noted that Hitler's fear of being poisoned only came about after the transformation of his character at the end of the war.

> '... it might be that while he was fantasizing about what the victors might do to the vanquished when they arrived, his masochistic and perverse tendencies conjured up the thought that they might attack him and force him to eat dung and drink urine (a practice which, it is alleged, is fairly common in Nazi concentration camps).'

While he would get a certain masochistic pleasure from this, it also aroused feelings of guilt and disgust, a suicidal depression. To save himself, he must rid himself of his conscience and the dictates of the intellect. Having freed himself, he was left almost entirely at the mercy of his passions, instincts and unconscious desires. The result was the hallucination where an inner voice told him that he was going to redeem the German people and lead them to greatness. This confirmed the feeling from childhood that he was the 'chosen one' protected by providence so that he could fulfil a divine mission. Fate had sent him to Vienna to take the 'milk-sop out of him by giving him Dame Sorrow as a foster mother', he said.

IDENTIFICATION WITH THE AGGRESSOR

It seemed fate was stripping him of his identification with his mother – his 'humanity' – ridding him of this weakness because it was a 'law of nature' that the strong should dominate the weak. He now fantasized that he was a superman, surpassing his enemies in 'virile' qualities. This mechanism was called 'identification with the aggressor'. All his inferiorities, insecurities and guilt were negated and turned into their opposites, while all the human qualities of love, pity, sympathy and compassion were seen as weakness and banished in the transformation.

The old personality was projected on to some external object which the new personality was struggling against. In Hitler's case, this external object was the Jews, who became in his mind evil incarnate. He hated them with the same intensity that he had hated his former self.

Germany was now as weak, humiliated, passive and confused as he had once been. But providence had provided the means to change himself overnight. Now it was his mission to transform the German people in the same way, with the Jews being the repository of all the effeminate, masochistic and perverse elements that had dogged his former life.

Many observers assumed that Hitler simply used anti-Semitism for its propaganda value. But the sources Langer interviewed confirmed that Hitler had a sincere hatred for the Jews and everything Jewish.

'Just as Hitler had to exterminate his former self in order to get the feeling of being great and strong, so must Germany exterminate the Jews if it is to attain its new glory,' said Langer. This was written before any of the death camps had been liberated and the full extent of Hitler's mass murder programme became clear.

HITLER'S REASONS FOR EXTERMINATING THE JEWS

1. To appear to the world to be the pitiless brute he imagined himself to be
2. To prove to himself that he was as brutal and heartless as he wanted to be
3. To rid himself, and Germany, of what he believed to be the 'poison' responsible for all difficulties
4. As a masochist, he derived vicarious pleasure from the suffering of others
5. To give vent to his bitter hatred of the world by using the Jews as a scapegoat
6. It paid heavy material and propagandist dividends

TRANSFORMED PERSONALITY

Having transformed his personality, Hitler soon had an opportunity to display his ruthlessness. He spied on his comrades and reported those who voiced communist sentiments. At their trials he would give testimony that would send them to their deaths. His oratory then earned him a promotion. His invention of the new Hitler was paying dividends.

Langer said that 'identification with the aggressor' was, at best, an unstable form of adjustment. To banish unease, the person must prove themselves over and over again to be the type of person they had chosen to be.

'The result is a snow-ball effect. Every brutality must be followed by a greater brutality, every violence by greater violence, every atrocity by a greater atrocity, every gain in power by a greater gain in power, and so on down the line. Unless this is achieved successfully, the individual begins to feel insecure and doubts concerning his borrowed character begin to creep in together with feelings of guilt regarding his shortcomings. This is the key to an understanding of Hitler's actions since the beginning of his political activities to the present day.'

To support his arguments he quoted André François-Poncet, who said that Hitler was aware that the anti-Jewish persecutions of Kristallnacht in November 1938 were an enormous blunder, but he was still preparing a merciless attack on the Church and Catholicism.

'Perhaps he thus wishes to wipe out the memory of past violence with fresh violence,' François-Poncet said.

As the individual concerned could never convince themselves that they were secure, they had no choice but to plunge madly on. In rapid succession, Hitler joined the nascent Nazi Party, seized control of it, rapidly expanded its membership and introduced a reign of terror. Following a series of broken promises, collusions and betrayals, Hitler thought he was strong enough to seize power in a putsch in 1923. Langer was particularly interested in Hitler's reaction when it failed.

'Some report that when the troops fired on them Hitler fell to the ground and crawled through an alley which carried him to safety while Ludendorff, Röhm and Göring marched ahead.

Some claim that he stumbled, others that he was knocked down by his bodyguard who was killed. The Nazi version is that he stopped to pick up a small child who had run out into the street and been knocked down! Years later, they produced a child on the anniversary of the event to prove the story!'

Langer concluded that he turned coward at that moment because he did not have enough faith in his new character to test it in physical combat. Afterwards, he went into a deep depression and threatened suicide. In Landsberg prison he went on hunger strike for three weeks. He was back in the position of victim again. It was only when he found that his jailers were not unkindly disposed to him that he could be persuaded to take food.

'Landsberg had done him a world of good,' said Ludecke. 'Gone from his manner was the nervous intensity which formerly had been his most unpleasant characteristic.'

While there he wrote *Mein Kampf*. Langer said this gave him an opportunity to integrate his new character more firmly.

PROJECTED INSECURITIES

As Hitler rose to power, each successful step convinced him that he was the person he believed himself to be, but this still brought him no real sense of security. So the terror, violence and ruthlessness continued to increase. After he seized total power in Germany, he projected his insecurities into the surrounding nations. The course for war was set and victory had to be won at all costs.

His famous rages appeared at first to be a reaction to frustration. But when he was confronted with a real frustration such as failing to be elected president or be offered the chancellorship, he fell silent and immediately laid plans for a new attempt. The temper tantrums only occurred when his superman image was challenged. As soon as the rage had done its job and cowed listeners into submission, it was turned off.

'How great is the insecurity which demands such constant vigilance and apprehensions,' said Langer.

The same insecurity was in play when he came into contact with someone he felt inferior to. He would then try to overpower them with his status. If that failed, he would look at the ceiling for the rest of the interview.

He acted much the same if challenged in an argument. Strasser said: 'He evades the issue and ends up by throwing in your face an argument entirely remote from what you were talking about.'

As any defeat might mar his image of himself, he could not face any opposition. If he sensed that a group might oppose him, he simply walked out on his audience. Similarly, his procrastination was fear of coming to grips with any difficult problem. Only when he risked possible defeat and humiliation would he act and all his thinking was carried out on the unconscious level.

'Psychological experiments in this field seem to indicate that on this level the individual is often able to solve very complex problems which are impossible for him on the level of consciousness,' said Langer.

Hitler further compensated for his lack of confidence by constructing huge buildings, stadiums, bridges and roads. They proved his greatness both to himself and to others, though he constantly planned to replace them with even greater monuments.

His buildings were always surrounded by huge columns.

'Since pillars of this sort are almost universally considered to be phallic symbols, we may regard the size and frequency as unconscious attempts to compensate for his own impotence,' said Langer. 'His huge pageants served a similar purpose.'

APPEALING TO THE UNCONSCIOUS

His oratory was another example of his 'identification with the aggressor', allowing him to play out his superman role. Jews, the Bolsheviks, capitalist, liberal democracies were all built up, only to be knocked down again. The audience, he said, was feminine by nature and Hitler, a man who never uttered a profanity offstage, poured into the heads of his listeners a stream of curses, foul names, vilification and hatred until he was pouring with sweat in, what many observers remarked, was a veritable orgasm.

This, Langer pointed out, was a reversal of his masochistic perversion where he found gratification in having women pour their filth on him. His mouth, which he usually protected from contamination, then became the organ through which filth was ejected. Hitler's rants were described as 'verbal diarrhoea'. Rauschning called them an oral enema.

'It is probably this unconscious sexual element in his speaking which holds such a fascination for many people,' said Langer.

He found that in many German people there was a feminine-masochistic element that was covered by more 'virile' characteristics, but found partial gratification in submissive behaviour – discipline and sacrifice – which was compensated for by going to the other extreme of courage; pugnaciousness, determination and the like.

Hitler could appeal directly to this. All he had to do was dwell on the longings, hopes and desires he had had in his earlier life, then take them through his own transformation, twinning them to his new view of life which stressed brutality, ruthlessness, dominance and determination, while banishing all humanitarian qualities. The aim was to strive to be what you were not, while destroying all that you were.

Langer commented:

'The behaviour of the German armies has been an outstanding manifestation of this contradiction. To the psychologist it seems as though the brutality expressed towards the people of the occupied countries is motivated not only by a desire to prove to themselves that they are what they are not, but also by vicarious masochistic gratification which they derive from an identification with their victims.'

Langer concluded his analysis of Hitler with a quotation from Rauschning: 'There lies behind Hitler's emphasis on brutality and ruthlessness the desolation of a forced and artificial inhumanity, not the amorality of a genuine brute, which has after all something of the power of a natural force.'

Of the German people, Langer said that by playing on their unconscious tendencies Hitler had paralyzed their critical functions and assumed that role for himself. He had incorporated himself into the personalities of his individual supporters and so could dominate their mental processes. This lay at the heart of the bond between Hitler and his people. In fighting for Hitler, they were fighting for their own psychological integrity.

In a carefully orchestrated ceremony, Hitler takes credit for a new autobahn in 1935; Pathe News sent moving images around the world.

SUICIDE

Like Murray, Langer also concluded his study with a series of predictions about Hitler's future actions: 'Hitler: His Probable Behaviour in the Future'. The possibility of Hitler dying of natural causes was remote. He seemed to be in good health, except for his stomach ailment which was probably psychosomatic. It was also unlikely that he would seek refuge in a neutral country, something he had often condemned the Kaiser for doing at the end of World War I.

If he became convinced he could not win, he might well seek death in battle. This would inspire his followers to fight fanatically to the bitter end and ensure his immortality in legend.

Hitler himself was afraid of assassination. If done by a friend, this would again make him the stuff of legend. If done by a Jew, it would ensure the massacre of those still surviving.

He might go insane. Faced with defeat, his psychological structure might collapse completely, though this was less likely as he grew older.

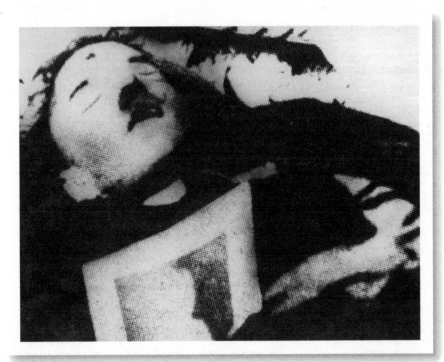

Photograph of a corpse reputed to have been found near Hitler's bunker in 1945; it wasn't Hitler though.

However, it was a desirable outcome as it would undermine the Hitler legend in the minds of the German people.

It was unlikely that his own troops would turn on him. But if he became increasingly neurotic in the face of defeat it might be necessary for the military to confine him. It would be unlikely that the German people would be told though. Although it would make sense to dethrone him and sue for peace, this would cause internal strife and Langer considered the possibility extremely remote. It seemed to him even more unlikely that Hitler would fall into Allied hands.

The most plausible outcome, Langer decided, was that Hitler would commit suicide. Langer concluded by saying:

'In any case, his mental condition will continue to deteriorate. He will fight as long as he can with any weapon or technique that can be conjured up to meet the emergency. The course he will follow will almost certainly be the one which seems to him to be the surest road to immortality and at the same time wreaks the greatest vengeance on a world he despises.'

And that, of course, was what happened.

FURTHER READING

Baynes, H.G., *Germany Possessed*, Jonathan Cape, London, 1941

Bromberg, Norbert and Small, Verna Volz, *Hitler's Psychopathology*, International Universities Press, New York, 1983

Dietrich, Otto, *The Hitler I Knew: Memoirs of the Third Reich's Press Chief*, Skyhorse Publishing, New York, 2014

Fest, Joachim C., *Hitler*, Penguin Books, London, 1974

Heiden, Konrad, *Führer*, Skyhorse Publishing, New York, 2012

Hitler, Adolf, *Hitler's Table Talk, 1941–1944* (with an introductory essay 'The Mind of Adolf Hitler' by H.R. Trevor-Roper), Weidenfeld and Nicolson, London, 1953

Humphreys, P. Callon, *Mind of a Tyrant: A Psychological Study of the Character of Hitler*, Gordon & Gotch, London, 1940

Junge, Traudl, *Hitler's Last Secretary*, Arcade Publishing, New York, 2011

Kempka, Erich, *I Was Hitler's Chauffeur: The Memoir of Erich Kempka*, Frontline Books, Barnsley, South Yorkshire, 2012

Kershaw, Ian, *Hitler*, Penguin, London, 2009

Langer, William L., *The Mind of Adolf Hitler: The Secret Wartime Report*, Pan Books, London, 1974

Linge, Heinz, *With Hitler to the End: The Memoirs of Adolf Hitler's Valet*, Skyhorse Publishing, New York, 2014

Ludecke, Kurt, *I Knew Hitler: The Lost Testimony by a Survivor from the Night of the Long Knives*, Pen & Sword Military, Barnsley, South Yorkshire, 2013

Misch, Rochus, *Hitler's Last Witness: The Memoirs of Hitler's Bodyguard*, Frontline Books, Barnsley, South Yorkshire, 2014

Rauschning, Hermann, *The Beast from the Abyss*, William Heinemann, London, 1941

Rauschning, Hermann, *Hitler Speaks: A Series of Political Conversations with Adolf Hitler on His Real Aims*, Kessinger Publishing, Whitefish, Montana, 2010

Rauschning, Hermann, *The Voice of Destruction*, Pelican Publishing Company, Gretna, Louisiana, 2003

Redlich, Fritz, *Hitler: Diagnosis of a Destructive Prophet*, Oxford University Press, Oxford, 1999

Rees, Laurence, *The Dark Charisma of Adolf Hitler: Leading Millions into the Abyss*, Ebury Press, London, 2012

Schroeder, Christa, *He Was My Chief: The Memoirs of Adolf Hitler's Secretary*, Frontline Books, Barnsley, South Yorkshire, 2012

Schwaab, Edleff H., *Hitler's Mind: A Plunge into Madness*, Praeger Publishers, New York, 1992

Strasser, Otto, *Hitler and I*, Jonathan Cape, London, 1940

Victor, George, *Hitler: The Pathology of Evil*, Brassey, Washington, 2000

Von Below, Nicolaus, *At Hitler's Side: The Memoirs of Hitler's Adjutant*, Frontline Books, Barnsley, South Yorkshire, 2010

Waite, Robert G.L., *The Psychopathic God: Adolf Hitler*, Da Capo Press, Boston, 1993

INDEX

PICTURE CREDITS